LINCOLN CHRISTIAN UNIVERSITY P9-DDX-564

LINGUISTICS
for
L2 TEACHERS

LINGUISTICS
for
L2 TEACHERS

Larry Andrews
University of Nebraska—Lincoln

Routledge
Taylor & Francis Group
New York   London

Routledge is an imprint of the
Taylor & Francis Group, an informa business

Copyright © 2001 by Lawrence Erlbaum Associates, Inc.
All rights reserved. No part of this book may be repro-
duced in any form, by photostat, microfilm, retrieval
system, or any other means, without prior written permission of the publisher.

First Published by Lawrence Erlbaum Associates, Inc., Publishers
10 Industrial Avenue
Mahwah, New Jersey 07430

Reprinted 2008 by Routledge

Routledge
Taylor and Francis Group
270 Madison Avenue
New York, NY 10016

Routledge
Taylor and Francis Group
2 Park Square
Milton Park, Abingdon
Oxon OX14 4RN

Cover design by Kathryn Houghtaling Lacey

Library of Congress Cataloging-in-Publication Data
Andrews, Larry.
Linguistics for L2 teachers / Larry Andrews.
p. cm.
Includes bibliographical references and indexes.
ISBN 0-8058-3818-X (pbk. : alk. paper)
1. Language and languages—Study and teaching.
2. English language—Study and teaching—Foreign
speakers. 3. Applied linguistics. I. Title.
P53 .A573 2001
428'.0071—dc21   00-056214
                                          CIP

In memoriam
Conrad Stawski
A. Sterl Artley
Alvah Kilgore

248/96

113166

Contents

5 AMERICAN ENGLISH VARIATIONS   **87**

Preface

Teachers of English to students who are learning English as a new language face numerous challenges frequently unknown to the other teachers in the school building.

To begin with, in elementary schools there are teachers who have followed courses of study, at the undergraduate level and often at the graduate level, learning how to help native English-speaking children learn how to read and write, how to do math, science, art, and the like.

Moreover, in middle schools and high schools there are teachers who have followed similar courses of study in order to learn how better to teach history, geography, English, music, and other subjects to native English-speaking learners. Usually, these teachers declared an academic major in these subjects during their university studies.

Teachers of English to those children whose languages of nurture were not English come to English as a second language

(ESL) and bilingual classrooms, however, often following very different teacher-training routes.

Many school districts in the United States have experienced significant growth in the numbers of ESL students who lack sufficient proficiency in oral or written English in order to succeed in school; consequently, as the schools attempt to provide for the needs of these learners, they also need to find teachers who can help the second-language learners to learn.

School principals, faced with the need to staff an ESL classroom *immediately*, look at their faculty rosters for a possible solution: They ask themselves, "Who's on the faculty who will take on this challenge?" Or, the need for an ESL teacher might be announced at a general faculty meeting: The principal asks, "Is there a volunteer?"

From the ranks of teachers of Spanish, French, and German; speech pathologists, school counselors, reading teachers, math teachers, traditionally trained "mainstream" teachers, an ESL teacher is usually found and is assigned to teach an ESL class.

Despite the increase in the number of teacher-training programs for teachers of students for whom English is a new language, many ESL and bilingual teachers today have, understandably, had no or little professional education in ESL pedagogy, in cross-cultural communication, or in the English language.

Many ESL and bilingual teachers were "something else" first. With my tongue firmly fixed in my cheek, I once included the following sentence in a speech: "Many ESL and bilingual teachers and Unitarians have at least one characteristic in common: not many started out to be one."

Understand, I am not faulting these teachers; to the contrary, I think they are to be admired.

Because many ESL or bilingual teachers have not studied the English language, its properties, features, conventions, and its varying uses for varying purposes, I have written this text.

My hope is that after having had the opportunity to read this book—either as a textbook in a formal university course or in a more informal, continuing education or staff-development setting—ESL and bilingual teachers will better understand and appreciate how and why the English language works. With that better understanding and appreciation, they will be better prepared to meet the important challenges and questions they encounter.

This text is not a complete curriculum in English linguistics. It is, rather, a foundation from which the professional ESL or bilingual educator, and, therefore, his or her students, can continue to grow and to teach with greater confidence.

HOW THIS TEXT IS ORGANIZED

Several educators have told me that they have enjoyed using one of my textbooks, *Language Exploration and Awareness* (Andrews, 1998), in their teacher-training programs. That text, they tell me, provides a good introduction to aspects of language for the prospective or in-service ESL or bilingual teacher, but because the text is intended for K–12 English language arts teachers, they skip several chapters.

In response to suggestions from these teacher-educators, I have written *Linguistics for L2 Teachers.* This text attempts to provide basic aspects of language study, especially for teachers of ESL and bilingual learners.

Each chapter begins with a prereading activity, labeled "As You Approach This Chapter." Ideally, you'll have an opportunity to discuss the questions in the prereading activities either with a colleague or with members of a university or staff-development class. The research supporting the uses of prereading activities is relatively clear: They help the reader to activate and focus what he or she already knows about the contents of the reading selection, thereby enhancing both comprehension and understanding.

Similarly, each chapter concludes with a postreading activity called "For Discussion." I invite you to think about the statements and questions in these activities, making notes to yourself when appropriate. Even better, I hope you will have the opportunity to discuss your responses to the postreading activities with others.

The postreading activities are created in two forms that will be familiar to those with experience in reading pedagogy. Some postreading activities are three-level reading guides and some are question–answer–relationship (Q–A–R) strategies. In the postreading activities you will be asked to respond either to declarative statements or to questions that elicit responses at the explicit, implicit, and schema- or experienced-based levels of comprehension.

If you are not familiar with these activities, please be patient with them the first time you use them. The research on these strategies is relatively conclusive, too: They help readers clarify their understanding of a reading selection and they help readers to respond to a reading selection at increasingly higher levels of comprehension.

Each chapter also has one or two activities titled "Be a Linguist." I have tried to make these activities interactive and I hope they will help you to think in ways similar to the ways linguists think. These activities will give you an opportunity to apply some of the concepts explained in the chapter.

TERMINOLOGY

First, you will notice that this text has no glossary. I have tried to keep the technical terminology to a minimum and I introduce it, only when necessary, in **boldface type** and in a meaningful context. This is how you encounter new words in real life.

Second, throughout the text I use the acronym *ENL* instead of the more familiar acronym *ESL*.

ESL, English as a second language, assumes that English is the *second* language the learners are acquiring. This is often a misleading idea. Many of them are learning English as a third or, perhaps, a fourth language. Consequently, I prefer to use *ENL*, English as a new language. It is more accurate, I believe.

Third, using either acronym, ESL or ENL, is a convention writers in this field of endeavor use, but I don't like to label people any more than you do. So, when you read about either an *ESL* or an *ENL* learner, remember we're talking about real people, like Svetlana, Carlos, Nga, or Mohammed.

ACKNOWLEDGMENTS

Although I am listed as the author of this text, books are seldom completed in isolation.

I'm grateful to the University of Nebraska—Lincoln (UN–L) for providing me with uninterrupted time for writing. Thanks to Jim O'Hanlon, dean of the UN–L Teachers College, and Elizabeth A. Franklin, chair of the Department of Curriculum and Instruction, for their support.

My secretary, Diane Ohlson (you'll meet her as "The Dutiful Diane" in the text), attended to many telephone calls and e-mail messages diverted from my desk to hers during my leave of absence, and she demonstrated, again, why she's so important.

I am fortunate in that I have had bright and dedicated preservice and in-service teachers in my classes and in my life. Through their nudging, badgering, and questioning, they have helped me to understand better many aspects of language I thought I was certain about. From them, I have learned much.

This is the third textbook I have published following the guidance of Naomi Silverman. Naomi is a consummate professional and brings luster to the publishing field. I am grateful for her continuing encouragement, support, wisdom, and guidance.

Lori Hawver, assistant editor at Lawrence Erlbaum Associates, is a gem. She managed all the details associated with the creation of this text with precision and good humor; thank you, Lori.

I appreciate the pre-publication critique from Christian Faltis, Arizona State University, which helped me to bring this book to you with clearer and more accurate writing.

I am grateful to my wife, Ruthie, my most severe and my most loving critic. Not only did she help to prepare the copy for this text, but, even more significantly, she was always *there* when I either knowingly or unknowingly needed her, especially when I was brooding and pacing because I had written myself either into a corner, up a tree, or down a creek. Her patience, support, and encouragement have been and continue to be important and constant.

—*Larry Andrews*

Introduction

A couple of summers ago, my older daughter and I went to Bolivia to visit my younger daughter who was living in Cochabamba, teaching English at a secondary school in the mornings and working at a day-care center in the afternoons.

When we attempted to board the airplane for the final leg of our journey, we were stopped at the gate at the La Paz airport by a young man wearing an army uniform, an Uzi slung over his shoulder. I showed him our airline tickets and boarding passes, but he stopped us and said "No! Tasa!" I pushed the tickets and boarding passes closer to him, hoping he would recognize the fact that we were authorized to board.

The young man yelled in a louder voice, "NO! TASA!"

I was equally bewildered and intimidated by the young man's demeanor and his Uzi. My older daughter was green with altitude sickness and was, by no fault of hers, no help. I was desperate. We can't stay in La Paz forever, I told myself. What are we going to do? I felt powerless. We needed help.

A *Norte Americano* standing behind us came to the rescue. "He's telling you," she said, "that you have to pay the airport tax."

Before beginning our journey I had rehearsed some essential survival sentences: *Una cerveza, por favor*, and *Taza de café con leche, por favor*. I knew *taza* was Spanish for "cup." What I didn't know was its homonym, *tasa*, "tax."

I paid the tax and we were on our way.

I have traveled abroad many times, so I know how to find my way around airports in other countries. I've studied Spanish and thought my proficiency in it would enable me to be a successful communicator with the native speakers. I'm old enough that I have encountered obstacles before and I know, or thought I knew, how to find other doors or paths. But, despite these experiences, everything broke down in the La Paz airport.

How often do immigrant and refugee children and adults who are new to the United States have similar experiences? (Although teachers in U.S. schools don't carry Uzis!) Lacking proficiency in English, they often feel powerless, intimidated, bewildered, and lost.

Every time I am in a classroom filled with learners for whom English is a new language, I am astonished when I think about how much language-learning is ahead of them. I am also amazed at how quickly many of them learn English!

I wrote this book for those learners, believing that the more their teachers know about American English, the more students will learn.

This book reflects my personal view of American English. Despite the fact that I rely on the scholarship of others throughout the text, as noted in the endnotes, the contents describe my notions about people and language.

For example, I do not believe American English is a "thing," an entity, a physical object. Of course, we can record American English through writing, or on video- or audiotapes, but when we do that, we haven't made a record of what's going on in the heads of the language users and we usually cannot document the multiple situations or contexts in which authentic language is used.

This book does not present new ways to diagram sentences so that ENL or bilingual students can better learn American English grammar. To the contrary, the view in this book sees language as a human activity in which the users make decisions about language options that are available to them, and these choices are shaped by their purposes for communicating, their native culture, their new culture, and their immediate context.

Several aspects of American English are presented in this text, not just grammar and usage. As you, an ENL, a bilingual, or a foreign language teacher become more proficient in your command of a variety of aspects of American English, your students will become more proficient as well.

As you start this book, I stop. I have done my work; the rest is up to you. I can't depart, however, without recalling the words of Ludwig Wittgenstein: *the limits of my language are the limits of my universe.* Please consider what his words can mean, both for you, a teacher of English, and for your students who are learning English.

CHAPTER 1

Some Basic Features
of Language and Communication

Somehow the mystery of language
was revealed to me. I knew that
"w-a-t-e-r" meant that wonderful cool
something that was flowing over my hand.
—Helen Keller, *The Story of My Life*

As you approach this chapter, think about how
giving directions and participating in "party talk"
are different types of language use; given these two
distinctions, how does what you have learned over
the years help you to be a successful communicator?
Also, in how many ways is the language you use
different from the communication systems animals
use?

A BRIEF INTRODUCTION

The purpose of this book is to help the teacher of those learners for whom English is a new language (ENL). For some readers, the contents of this text will be new information; other readers will find the text a useful review of previously learned ideas about the English language.

At the beginning, I would like to make one thing very clear: This is not a textbook describing teaching methods and strategies to use in ENL and bilingual classrooms. Rather, this is a textbook designed specifically for the ENL or bilingual teacher who has had limited opportunities to study the English language.

I don't know whether you consider yourself a language expert, but many do, or will, depending on where you are on your professional career ladder. Your colleagues at school, your ENL students, and often the parents of your students believe that you are an authority—sometimes *the* authority—when it comes to questions about how and why American English works the way it does. When you have completed this text, your proficiency as an American English language authority will be greater, trust me. (I say this despite one of my favorite lines from the play, *Steel Magnolias*: "Don't ever trust a man who says 'Trust me.'")

I have two more caveats to offer, then we'll get down to our business.

First, there are two subdivisions within the field of linguistics that are important for the ENL teacher to understand: psycholinguistics and sociolinguistics. **Psycholinguistics** merges the studies of psychology and linguistics and typically examines topics such as language acquisition, neurolinguistics (language and the brain), brain damage, and aphasia. **Sociolinguistics**, on the other hand, examines how language actually works in the world, in society, and how language users adapt their uses of language to different social contexts.

There are several good texts addressing psycholinguistic issues important to ENL teachers; there is no need for those works to be duplicated. There are also any number of grammar texts available for those ENL teachers who want or need more information about English grammar.

The ideas in this text are presented from a sociolinguistic perspective, examining how English works in society. From time to time, you'll read a psycholinguistic description or observation, because a merged perspective between the two approaches seems appropriate. Nevertheless, the predominate viewpoint or attitude will be a sociolinguistic one. Learners for whom English is a new language must learn certain standard uses of English, but ultimately they will need to use English, to the best of their ability, as it is used by native English speakers in the local, or host culture. If they don't or can't, then their successes in school, at work, at the mall, or anywhere else where English is the dominant language will be in serious jeopardy.

The second caution can be described more briefly. I hope you have examined why you want to be an ENL teacher and why, in your schooled opinion, immigrant and refugee children and adults need to learn English. So that you'll know me better (and not because you must agree with me), let me describe my position. I believe immigrant and refugee children and adults should learn English because the degree to which they become more proficient in the language of their new country, the wider the range of options available to them in their lives. The better they can use English, the more options they will have available to them.

I do not believe English is inherently "better" than the ENL learner's native language. I am not a linguistic imperialist. I am, on the other hand, an educator who believes strongly that one of my first obligations to my students is to help them to develop as wide a range of alternatives, options, and choices their expertise will allow. Our job, as I see it, is to help our students gain the linguistic abilities that will enable them to open more doors.

SOME NUANCES OF COMMUNICATION

I want to begin this chapter by borrowing a story from Richard Lederer, a writer who has written several popular books about English (and a delightful dinner companion, I might add).

Quasimodo, the hunchback of Notre Dame Cathedral, having grown too old to ring the bell in the tower, placed a classified ad in the local newspaper searching for a replacement.

A man with no arms appeared at the door. Quasimodo asked, "Have you come to inquire about the bell-ringing job?" "Indeed, I have," the man answered.

Somewhat non-pulsed, Quasimodo asked, "How can you ring the bell with no arms?" "It's easy," the man replied. "Although I have no arms, I have a tough skull. I run at the bell and butt it with my forehead."

Quasimodo hired the man, admiring his superlative perseverance.

The new bell-ringer climbed the stairs, ran at the bell, butted it with his forehead, and a lovely tone sounded. However, when the bell returned, in pendulum fashion, it smashed into the armless man and knocked him to the cobblestone street far below.

When the police arrived an officer asked, "Do you know this man?"

"Yes, he worked for me," answered Quasimodo.

The police officer continued, "Can you give me the man's name? We need to notify his next of kin."

"I don't know his name," Quasimodo said, "but his face rings a bell."[1]

◇◇◇◇◇

A second chapter in this story involves the twin brother of the armless man, hired for the same job, who meets the same fate! Quasimodo tells the police this unfortunate soul is a *dead ringer* for his brother!

These puns play on expressions that have two or more meanings. Although these stories are offered in the spirit of fun, you can imagine, I'm sure, how either expression, "rings a bell" or "dead ringer," might *not* communicate humor (such as it is) to a learner for whom English is a new language. These learners face zillions of nuances about the language they are trying to learn!

THE ORIGIN OF LANGUAGE

In one of the courses I teach, we begin and end with the same question: "Where did language come from?" Whether our topic is the origin of language or the history of English, the question, although redundant, seems appropriate in both places.

I am not the only writer about language who has made the following confession about where language comes from: No one really knows.

Which language is the oldest one? Did all languages evolve from a single source? Which language was used in the Garden of Eden? In the beginning, how were words created?

These are engaging questions and they have been asked, as best we can tell, for some 3,000 years! Each generation, it seems, keeps asking these questions, with the same frustrations of earlier generations. We have very little knowledge and evidence to use in answering these questions. The questions, nevertheless, keep appearing. All we can do is speculate.

Indeed, one group of 19th-century scholars was so dissatisfied (and perhaps bored) with these questions that they took severe action: the Linguistic Society of Paris, in 1866, published an edict banning discussions about the origins of language at their meetings.[2] So much for the open exchange of ideas at meetings of scholarly societies!

Otto Jespersen, a Danish linguist ("the great Dane," 1869–1943) collected a number of origins of language theories, offered here for your amusement. As you read about these theories, referred to here by their nicknames, please remember this: No matter how comical a theory might sound to you, today's 21st-century reader, each theory had a number of adherents at an earlier time.

The "Bow-Wow" Theory. Oral language began when people tried to imitate the sounds they heard in their environment, especially animal sounds or calls. The primary evidence supporting this theory, apparently, is the use of **sound symbols**, commonly known as **onomatopoeic words**. From the environment, then, words like *hiss, bow-wow, click, creak, rustle, boom,* and so on, came in to the language.

It is a fact that most languages in the world have onomatopoeic words, but it is also a fact that onomatopoeic words vary considerably in the ways they are used to represent sounds. It is also a fact that onomatopoeic words constitute an extremely small percentage of the total number of words available for use—in either written or oral form—in any language's vocabulary. My advice, therefore, is don't bet a prized possession on this theory.

The "Pooh-Pooh" Theory.   Advocates of this theory hypothesized that people instinctively make sounds caused by pain, anger, and other human emotions. The primary evidence supporting this theory is, apparently, the universal use of sounds as interjections, like *gosh,* or *gasp.* These words are rare in most languages, and the sounds made when you suddenly inhale from fright bear little relationship to the vowels and consonants used in the words you and I use. To this theory, I'd say pooh-pooh.

The "Ding-Dong" Theory.   According to this theory, speech was created when people reacted to certain stimuli in their environment and they produced, spontaneously, sounds ("oral gestures") that in some way demonstrated that they were in tune with the environment. Some dreamlike examples include the word *mama,* a word reflecting how the lips move then approaching the mother's breast. Similarly, the words *bye-bye* and *ta-ta* demonstrate, ostensibly, how the lips and tongue work when we wave "good-bye" to someone. Please explain to me how the expression "Life, liberty, and the pursuit of happiness" supports this theory.

The "Yo-He-Ho" Theory.   Could it be, some have theorized, that language began when people worked together moving large objects, producing grunts, groans, and gasps? Their continued group efforts, with the accompanying and continuing grunts, groans, and gasps led to the creation of chants. The primary evidence in support of this theory is presence of **prosodic elements** (suprasegmental aspects of language: stress, pitch, and rhythm) in most of the world's languages. How these chants might have led to the totality of a complete language leaves too much to chance, in my view.[3]

The theorizing goes on today. As newer archaeological findings help to inform this discussion, we may learn more.

FEATURES OF COMMUNICATION

Of course, these theories sound either amusing or absurd today, but they represent earnest attempts to explain a history about which we know very little. What these theories have in common, I suggest, is the recurrence of people attempting to communicate with each other. The theorists recognized this basic feature of humanity. Communication is a social activity involving human beings acting in a collaborative activity, a theme found in all of the theories. Most of the conversations that are only imagined in these theories are, in fact, similar to conversations you participate in daily.

Some of your conversations are, for example, illustrative of the **interactional function** of language.[4] Interactional language is used primarily to establish and maintain social relations.

Last weekend, my wife and I attended a birthday party for a faculty colleague. A new member of the faculty and his wife were also in attendance. The conversations were light, breezy, and by definition, social; the conversational partners were demonstrating friendliness. Some of the interactional language I observed was about the weather ("You think this is hot? You should've been here last summer!"). Some of the conversations, especially with the new faculty member, were about neighborhoods ("Actually, I enjoy living in south Lincoln. There's that new shopping center at South 27th and Pine Lake Road, you know."). Other conversations were about sports ("Who's the better quarterback do you think, Bobby Newcombe or Eric Crouch?").

These subjects are fairly predictable conversational topics. Their primary purpose is to establish and maintain social bridges and relationships.

Transactional language, on the other hand, has a different purpose: to transmit knowledge, skills, or information.[5] Gillian Brown described transactional language as being *message-oriented* because its purpose is to create a change in the listener's knowledge.[6]

Transactional language is often heard at faculty meetings ("Let me tell you about our new procedures for ordering supplies.") and in classrooms ("When you want to retrieve a file from the archive, this is what you do ...").

These distinctions are important in classrooms in which there are learners for whom English is a new language. In teaching either conversation or listening comprehension, for example, it is important for both the teacher and the student to know the different purposes undergirding interactional and transactional language.[7]

Human communication can also be described as either **direct** (intentional) or **indirect** (inferential). Direct, intentional communications offer a smaller range in the *meaning potential* behind the expression.[8] Which is to say, by way of illustration, statements such as these provide few alternative understandings: "Norm caught a 5-pound, largemouth bass." "Sally lived in Israel for 6 months." "Ruthie works at the Pfizer Animal Health facility in Lincoln, Nebraska."

When the meaning potential provides more alternative understandings, by way of contrast, the communication is indirect, or inferential. If you observe, for example, that a friend is wearing one black sock and one brown sock, what are some possible meaning(s) you can ascribe to your observation? Your friend is a sloppy dresser? Your friend is colorblind? Your friend dressed in the dark? Your friend has a pile of dirty clothes and had only two unmatched but clean socks in the bureau drawer? Are there additional possibilities?

Direct communication is common, and it offers fewer challenges to ENL learners. Indirect communication is also relatively common but, on the other hand, it will offer greater challenges to understanding, especially when the communication involves metaphors or idiomatic expressions. For example, a student from a country where baseball is relatively unknown may have difficulty with either "You're way off base." or "You hit a homer on this assignment." Or, what might the ENL learner make out an encouraging teacher who advises the student to "take the bull by the horns?" When is an assignment "a piece of cake?" Do you need a camera to "get the picture?" This list of illustrations could be the longest part of this textbook, but I'll stop here. I think you get the picture.

> **Be a linguist.** For the next 2 or 3 days, observe the language you encounter at the mall, at school, while reading the newspaper, watching television, examining the mail you receive, and the like. How many examples can you find of: interactional and transactional language, and direct and inferential communication? How are these features of language uniquely *human*?

PROPERTIES OF LANGUAGE

Although communication is an intensely human activity, communication isn't limited to human beings. Animals communicate, too. Only yesterday I saw a person on the television network news who is convinced that her dog can say "I love my mama."

Frankly, I had trouble reconstructing "I love my mama" from the dog's yowls, but the dog's owner did not! She was as certain as only a pet-loving person can be.

Animals no doubt communicate with others of the same species and the media are full of reports like the dog just described. Many people, I have observed, are convinced that they and their pets have developed a capacity for encoding and decoding complicated messages. Therefore, as we begin to discuss how human communication differs from animal communication, please remember that I am not, of course, talking about *your* dog, cat, parakeet, or whatever. Rather, I'm talking about all of the *other* animals in the world.

Animal communication is, for the most part, very direct. If a dog goes to the door and barks sharply, there's not much room for alternative interpretations. The dog needs to go outside!

Similarly, a pet will signal when it is hungry, typically by first going to the place where it usually receives its food. At this place, the pet has been previously rewarded with food. Second, the pet might bark or meow, having been rewarded previously, following the bark or meow, with food. You can interpret these signals as you wish. I call them operant conditioning.

If you ask a pet dog, "Do you want Kibbles'n Bits again today?", you are likely to get the same bark, however. Dogs and other animals don't understand "again," meaning past practice, history. They communicate in the present, the here and now.

Humans, on the other hand, not only understand the concepts of history and of the future, but they can *talk* about last week, last year, 10 years ago, or next year. Human language transcends time and space.

This transcendent property is called **displacement**. Only human beings, it appears, have the capacity to talk about things that transcend *this* moment and *this* place.[9]

The honey bee apparently has the ability to return to the hive and communicate to the other bees—through a sophisticated "waggle" dance—the location of nectar, indicating both the direction and the distance of the nectar, demonstrating some degree of displacement, but the word *degree* must be emphasized. Ethologists—scientists who study innate, instinctive animal behavior—believe the honey bee can only refer to the most recent source of nectar, not a source found yesterday.[10]

Displacement is a very enabling characteristic of human language inasmuch as it describes our ability to think about, talk about, and share with others our ideas of the past and our hopes for the future. It enables us to interpret history and to speculate about the years ahead. It enables us to describe ideas and possibilities that are—at the communicative moment—contrary to fact.

Displacement suggests that human language is more symbolic than are animal signaling systems. Given this symbolic quality, human language can also be characterized by the property of being **arbitrary**, in that there is no direct relationship between a word and the thing the word refers to. If there were a direct relationship, than all languages would use the same word for the same referents. We know this isn't the case, however. A small amount of knowledge of other languages makes this clear: What is named a *dog* in English is named an *inu* in Japanese, a *perro* in Spanish, and a *sobaka* in Russian.[11]

Arbitrariness is a characteristic of human languages that you've understood for a long time, even if you haven't used the term. But, this property of human language has obvious restrictions. For example, if you decide you're tired of the word *book* and you're going to start referring to the objects previously called *books* by using the term *claxirs*, don't be surprised if people look at you as if you have trees growing out of your ears.

In human languages, then, symbols and the meanings ascribed to them are, generally, arbitrary. Animal signaling systems, on the other hand, have a set and fixed number of sounds available to them. This idea leads naturally to another important property of human language, that of **productivity**.

Humans can use the linguistic resources available to them in order to create new words, which enable them to encode new statements and new expressions.[12] The degree to which productivity is apparent in human language becomes even clearer when you consider the new words and expressions entering the vocabulary. Collegiate dictionaries, usually revised on a 10-year cycle, will list the words new to the most recent edition. You might also examine *The Atlantic Monthly* magazine; in alternate months of publication it has a column in which new word uses are discussed. (How new words and new meanings enter the language is discussed in much more detail in a later chapter.)

Animal languages do not possess productivity. A cicada, for example, has four fixed sounds, not five and not three. A vervet monkey has 36 signals it can emit, not 35 and not 37.[13] Given this aspect of permanence, these animals cannot change their systems of communications.

Neither the vervet monkey, the cicada, nor any other animal we might consider has the potential for the creation of new sounds or new strings of sound combinations and permutations. Human language, on the other hand, is anything but permanent; it is extraordinarily productive.

Some believe changes in the language demonstrate its vitality and vigor; others, on the other hand, do not. Jean Aitchison pointed out, for example, that any intelligent people might not only resent but they might also condemn languages changes, believing that they are symptomatic of human sloppiness, ignorance, or simple laziness.[14] This is not her attitude, but her observation.

We'll look at attitudes toward language change and variation in more detail when we discuss dialects and other variations. For the present, however, it must be emphasized that human language is unique because of its property of productivity. Whenever humans have a need for a new expression, they will create it.

Animal signals are not just permanently fixed, they are also universal within each species around the world. As you know, human languages are not universal, largely because of the property of **cultural transmission**.

Let's clarify cultural transmission by contrasting it with biological transmission. Through biological transmission we inherit the most visible features of our human biology: We inherit the color of our eyes, our hair color and texture, and our skin pigmentation from our parents, grandparents, and great grandparents.

No matter where you were born, how many times you've moved to another city, or where you are living at the present time, your physical features were biologically transmitted through the genes you inherited from your ancestors. This is a biological fact, but it cannot be confused with a linguistic fact: Language is not inherited; it is transmitted and learned from one's culture.[15]

I have been fortunate enough to have traveled in North America, South America, Africa, and Western Europe. I have heard dogs bark in Chicago, New York City, Atlanta, London, Cochabomba, Bolivia; Owerri, Nigeria; and in Amsterdam. The dogs didn't bark with different accents; the barks were the same. I can't say the same thing about the human languages I encountered in those same locations.

A generalization discussed several times in this book is that people usually talk *like* the people they talk *with*. Consequently, much of the pronunciation patterns, syntactical patterns, and word choices you make have been transmitted through the cultures you've been and are a part of.

One of my former students, I'll call him Tom, was born in Chiapas, Mexico. Tom was adopted by a couple in Chicago about 1 month after his birth. He grew up speaking English, because that's the language spoken by his adopted parents, their extended family, and their friends. Tom's birth parents were bilingual, speaking both a local language indigenous to Chiapas as well as Spanish. Tom did not inherit these languages from his birth parents; when I first knew him, he was taking a beginning Spanish language course. Language is transmitted and acquired through one's culture, not one's genes.[16]

More locally, you've no doubt observed any number of variations in the ways different people pronounce the same word: Some say *creek*, whereas others say *crick*, for example. Some say *skedule* and others might say *shedule*. Some say *greasy* and others say *greazy*.

People also use different words to denote the same object or concept. Do you go to "the movies" or to "the show"? Are the deceased interred in a "cemetery" or a "graveyard"? Do you wear "sneakers" or "tennies"? Would you prefer to drink a "milkshake" or a "cabinet"? Do you put perishable foods in the "refrigerator," the "fridge," or the "ice box"?

The choices made in these examples are shaped by one's culture. One choice is not especially better, from a linguistic point of view, than another. The language options we select are largely determined by the culture of which we are a part.

It is possible, furthermore, for us to distinguish between the vowel sounds in "creek" and "crick" or the consonant sounds in "pack" and "back" because the sounds in human language are meaningfully distinct, illustrating the property of **discreteness**. In human language, the sounds we use are discrete and separable.[17]

The actual differences you hear between the oral /p/ and the oral /b/ may seem insignificant to the ear, but they affect the meanings of *pack* and *back* and *pit* and *bit* enormously. The differences among these four illustrative words are derived from the ways we combine /p/ and /b/ with other symbols. Humans can separate these sounds and the corresponding symbols we use to represent those sounds. Animal sounds don't appear to be as separable.

> *Be a linguist.* Which of the properties of English are more or less important to you as distinguishing or critical attributes of human language? Why?

THE FIRST SUMMARY

This chapter has explored some of the basic building blocks of the English language, as well as some of the myths accounting for how language began. Throughout the remainder of this volume, I look at additional aspects of English and how they contribute to human communication in both formal classroom settings as well as in social settings. ENL students need to build their proficiency in both type of communication if they are to realize the range of choices and options described earlier in this chapter.

FOR DISCUSSION

Part 1. Place a ✓ in the space beside each statement found in this chapter.

___ 1. ENL students need to learn English so that they can get a job.
___ 2. Interactional language delivers directions.
___ 3. Animal signals transcend time, the here and now.
___ 4. Language change may be unfortunate, but it happens.
___ 5. We inherit language from our culture.

Part 2. Place a ✓ in the space beside each statement you believe the text would agree with. Please be prepared to explain your answers.

___ 6. Clear language use makes inferences unnecessary.

___ 7. Effective language use is always listener-oriented.
___ 8. Animal sounds seem to be species-specific.
___ 9. All language is open to interpretation.
___10. Language is special: Don't tinker with it.

Part 3. Based on what you know and what you have read in this chapter, place a ✓ beside each statement with which you can agree with. Please be prepared to explain your answers.

___11. If you think something is true, it might as well be true.
___12. Beauty is in the eye of the beholder.
___13. Nature is stronger than nurture.
___14. Form determines function; function doesn't determine form.
___15. I know what I like, and I like what I know.

NOTES

1. Richard Lederer, *The Miracle of English* (New York: Simon & Schuster Pocket Books, 1991), 38–39.
2. David Crystal, *The Cambridge Encyclopedia* of Language (2nd ed., Cambridge, England: Cambridge University Press, 1997), 290.
3. Ibid., 291.
4. Jack C. Richards, *The Language Teaching Matrix* (Cambridge, England: Cambridge University Press, 1990), 68. See also George Yule, *The Study of Language* (Cambridge, England: Cambridge University Press, 1985), 1.
5. Ibid.
6. Gillian Brown, "The Spoken Language," in Ronald Carter (ed.), *Linguistics and the Teacher* (London: Routledge & Kegan Paul, 1982), 75–76.
7. Richards, 68.
8. M. A. K. Halliday, *Learning How to Mean: Explorations in the Development of Language* (London: Edward Arnold, 1975), 37.
9. Charles F. Hockett, "Logical Considerations in the Study of Animal Communication," in Charles F. Hockett (ed.), *The View From Language* (Athens: The University of Georgia Press, 1977), 147.

10. Yule, 18.
11. Hockett, 142–143.
12. Yule, 19–20.
13. Ibid., 20.
14. Jean Aitchison, *Language Change: Progress or Decay?* (New York: Universe Books, 1985), 16.
15. Hockett, 155.
16. Yule, 21.
17. Hockett, 145.

Words and Dictionaries

"When I use a word," Humpty Dumpty said, in
a rather scornful tone, "it means just what I choose
it to mean. Nothing more nor less."
—Lewis Carroll, *Through the Looking Glass*

> **As you approach this chapter,** where do you think the words you use every day came from? Who created them? Why did they create them? Considering a related topic, what are the primary functions of a dictionary? People consult dictionaries every day. Why? What do they think they'll find there?

WORDS AND MORE MEANINGS

As you read in chapter 1, one of the properties of language unique to humans is the characteristic of **arbitrariness**. Humans are arbitrary when they assign a name to an entity, a referent, whether it's a person, place, thing, condition, or idea. Throughout the world, the same or similar objects have different names; even within the same language family in a given country, the same object, condition, or idea may have one name in one region, and another name in another region.

Nevertheless, all of us cannot speak with the authority of Humpty Dumpty. We can't change over night the ways words are typically and conventionally used in our language network. If we try to do so, we will be branded as deranged dupes or loonies.

Humpty Dumpty's remarks to Alice about words and their meanings reflect a controversy surrounding the relationship between words and meanings dating back to Plato's *Cratylus*.[1] In *Cratylus*, Plato examines the distinctions between two positions: words have a natural relationship to the objects they refer to in nature (*physis*), or words and their definitions are determined by convention (*nomos*), or by common consent.[2]

It is not in my stars to offer extended commentary here on Plato's dialogues, but you need to know, in fairness, that I opt for the *nomos* side of the argument. The meanings ascribed to words come from the people who use the words. A dictionary is a book that provides the history of which meanings have been used, both when, and often by whom.

Learning individual words is a major task for all language learners, especially when the language is English and the learner's first language is some other language. I say this because so many words in English are **polysemous** words, that is to say, they are words with multiple meanings and uses.

Take the word *pitch*, for example. One of the collegiate dictionaries in my study provides 14 separate meanings for *pitch*. It can mean the delivery of a baseball by a pitcher; a dark substance; the level or intensity of some state or condition ("feverish pitch"); resin obtained from trees, especially conifers; the level of a roof; a line of conversation used by someone who's trying to sell you something; a soccer or football field, and so on.[3] Maybe you can add to this list without using your dictionary.

How many meanings can you think of for the word *ring*? What about *run*? Try *school*, *class*, or almost any other common word. I don't think Humpty Dumpty was correct when he said a word means whatever he wants it to mean (arbitrariness can only go so far), but I do believe that English words can mean many different things, depending on the context in which the words is used.

Experienced ENL teachers, by the way, will be familiar with the admirable intentions of many of their students who bring their native language-to-English dictionaries with them to class. What these students must learn, however, is how to select the most appropriate definition, which often isn't the first definition listed under an entry word.

The supplements in Sunday newspapers frequently have articles about newer slang expressions, like *bag up* (to laugh really hard), *cubed out* (filled to capacity), *stroll* (to be out of prison on parole), *digerati* (the digital equivalent of literati), and *robo-anchor* (a television anchor person who reads the news but doesn't understand it).[4]

The electrification of our culture is contributing many *e-words*, patterned after *e-mail*. There's *e-cruiting* (recruiting employees on the Internet), *e-business*, *e-tailers*, and *e-commerce* (selling merchandise on the Internet). We also have *cyber-security* and *cyber-criminal*. There'll be an avalanche of *e*-words and *e*-related words, I predict. Some will remain in use and others will have a short life.

WHERE WORDS COME FROM

As you've seen, there have been several theories proposed in attempts to account for and understand better the creation of language. One theory we didn't include in our earlier discussion was the **Divine Origin Theory** because it specifically addresses word formation, a topic in this chapter.

In the Judeo-Christian tradition, God created language and Adam simultaneously. In Genesis 2:19 (RSV), we read that:

> God created every beast of the field and every bird of the air, and brought them to the man to see what he would call them; and whatever the man called every living creature, that was its name.

Given this Biblical assurance, the language used by Adam and Eve has been the subject of speculation. Andreas Kemke, a philologist proud (to the point of hubris) of his Swedish ancestry, was certain that God spoke the Swedish language. The first residents in the Garden of Eden, Adam and Eve, spoke Danish. The evil serpent spoke French.[5] Clearly, Kemke's travels to Copenhagen were more enjoyable than were his trips to Paris!

In another religious tradition, Hindu, words and language came from Sarasvati, wife of Brahma, the creator of the universe.[6] The Islamic tradition tells us, in *The Holy Qur'an*:

> And among His Signs Is the creation of the heavens and the earth, and the variations in your languages. . . .[7]

Let's examine the record of word *creation*. I suggest that word creation, the process of forming words, is relatively simple: Whenever a language network, a group of persons using the same language, need or want a new word, they will either create it or borrow it from another language.

For example, users of English have recently taken two existing words, *web* and *site*, in order to create a new compound word, *website*, a new concept. Remember when cars would *crash*? That existing word was given an additional meaning, and now computers *crash*, too. Consider also the newer computer-related meanings we associate with a word like *icon*, which entered the English language in the 16th century, or the word *mouse*, an Anglo-Saxon word dating back to the 12th century.

It is a relatively common practice for people to take an existing word and use it in a novel way, giving it an additional and a newer meaning. This doesn't mean, however, that an older meaning is more accurate. Believing this is an example of the **Etymological Fallacy**. For example, the word *decimate* originally meant to decrease by one tenth (see *dec-* in your dictionary). Today, *decimate* suggests total loss.

For another example, consider that the first recorded use of the word *hussy* dates back to 1505.[8] In the 16th century, *hussy* was a clipped form of the word *housewife* (more accurately, *huswif*). Nevertheless, I wouldn't recommend that you call a woman a *hussy* today, carefully explaining that you're using the word in its older, more accurate form. Similarly, the word *gossip*, an Anglo-Saxon word dating back before the 12th century, originally meant *godparent*.[9] *Gossip* doesn't mean *godparent* today, and to suggest that it does illustrates the Etymological Fallacy.

> *Be a linguist.* Let's investigate the Etymological Fallacy in more detail. Consider the meanings you ascribe to the following four words, then examine their etymologies in your dictionary. How significant are their changes in meaning? The four words are: *bonfire, lewd, minister,* and *steward.*

Not only do we use existing words in new ways, English speakers often borrow words from other languages. From Native American languages we have borrowed words like *chocolate, tomato, potato,* and *moose*.[10] Here are some additional words in the American English vocabulary, and the languages we borrowed them from: *aardvark* (Afrikaans); *mattress, algebra,* and *coffee* (Arabic); *bizarre* (Basque); *whiskey* and *plaid* (Celtic); *Santa Claus* (Dutch); *crappie, gopher,* and *pumpkin* (French).[11]

Other languages have been a source for words we use daily. Look at the names for the days of the week. *Wednesday,* the fourth day of the week, comes from the Anglo-Saxon *Odin's day* (Odin + daeg). Similarly, Thursday is also an Anglo-Saxon word, derived from *Thor's day* (Thursdaeg).

A similar process was involved in the naming of the months of the year. *July,* the seventh month, is derived from Latin and is named after Julius Caesar. The name *January* comes from the fact that the Romans dedicated the first month of the year to Janus. Consult your dictionary for the other names of the days of the week and the months of the year. It's fun to be a word nerd.

WORD-FORMATION PROCESSES

As already stated earlier in this chapter, words and the meanings ascribed to them come from *people*. Assuming this to be the case, what is it that people do when they form a new word?

By examining words in use, linguists have identified after the fact, *ex post facto*, how English words have been formed.

Coinage.   A coinage is a new word, a word never used before. This is one of the least used word formation processes and is quite common in the naming of products to be sold. *Aspirin*, for example, was initially a brand name for one, specific product, a fact you can validate by looking up this word in your dictionary where you'll find a definition complete with aspirin's chemical composition.[12] People have generalized the original meaning of *aspirin*, and today the word refers to a variety of pain-reducing, over-the-counter pills, tablets, and caplets.

Kleenex is another coinage, a totally new word, originally a brand name for one company's product. Like *aspirin*, *kleenex* has also become generalized, as you know, to refer to all brands of facial tissues.

Derivation.   Although coinage may be the rarest word-formation process, derivation may be the most common. Essentially, the derivation process enables people to create new words by building on the available stock of existing word parts, affixes.

For example, take the word *apply*. We can generate a new word by adding *mis-*, thereby creating *misapply*. In considering only a few prefixes and suffixes, like *un-*, *mis-*, *pre-*, *-ful*, *-less*, *-ish*, *-ism*, and *-ness*, just think of all the words we can create, like *unhook*, *prejudge*, *joyful*, *careless*, *boyish*, and *sadness*.

Borrowing.   This process was discussed earlier in this chapter. The English language has been enriched, as you've seen, by the number of borrowings from other languages. Whenever a people need a word for a new concept, they'll create the new word. How do you suppose we gained the word *pizza* in our all-American vocabulary.

There is a need for a new word today, and I have heard several alternatives, but there is no general agreement about these alternatives. In the days of rotary telephones, each telephone had a *dial* (noun), the circular arrangement of numbers at the base of each instrument. When people wanted to place a call, they would *dial* (verb) the desired number. My question is this: Because the noun *dial* seems to be an inappropriate word for today's touch-tone telephones, and because touch-tone telephone users don't really *dial* (verb) numbers, what new noun and verb will people select to refer to these aspects of telephone use?

Granted, my question isn't on the same level as how society can provide affordable health care for everyone, but it's a practical example.

I suspect a more honest term for **borrowing** might be *confiscation*. English has confiscated any number of words from other languages. No one, I suggest, asked any of the Arabic speaking countries if we could "borrow" the word *alcohol*. We simply appropriated it. We took it. Now, it's an English word. We did the same thing with *boss* (Dutch); *croissant* (French); *pretzel* (German); *yogurt* (Turkish); and, *zebra* (Bantu).

Several years ago, the Nebraska Unicameral (one house) legislature considered an amendment to the state constitution that would have established English as the state's "official" language. I opposed the proposed amendment and gave testimony against it. The proposal failed, not because of my testimony, I'm sure, but I'd like to think otherwise. Nevertheless, after the discussion and subsequent vote that defeated the proposal, I had some lapel buttons prepared that read: *Keep English Numero Uno*.

The buttons illustrated, I hoped, how borrowings from "foreign" languages have become a natural and normal part of the English language vocabulary.

Compounding.   This word-formation process is similar to **derivation**, with an important distinction. Instead of using word *parts*, compounding uses *whole* words and combines them. The word *blackbird* is a compound (obviously *black* + *bird*). In compounding, the newly formed word will be used as the same part of speech as the rightmost member. Reexamining *blackbird*, then, we have *black*, an adjective, conjoining with *bird*, a noun, creating a new noun, *blackbird*. This process is seen in many words like *highchair, bookcase, toothpaste, doorknob,* and *swearword*.[13]

Blending.   Blending creates new words through selective compounding. Whereas a compound word uses all of two preexisting words (e.g., *textbook*), blending uses only pieces of two preexisting words. An example of blending is the commonly used word *smog* (smoke + fog). A word that became popular with the proliferation of those 30- or 60-minute TV programs that are designed to look like programs but really are commercials is *infomercial* (*info*rmation + com*mercial*). Perhaps you know about the *chunnel* (*ch*annel + t*unnel*) linking Great Britain and France.

Clipping.   It is common practice for people to reduce words of two or more syllables, especially in casual speech and print media headlines and titles, to just one syllable. By clipping off a syllable or two, we derive *gas* from *gasoline, ad* from *advertisement, prof* from *professor*, and *bus* from *omnibus.*[14]

Acronym.   This word-formation procedure is another reduction process, like clipping, except that in creating an acronym people typically use only the first letter of each word in a series, thereby creating a new word. By taking the first letter of each word in *light amplification by stimulated emission of radiation,* we get *laser*. Similarly, from *self-contained underwater breathing apparatus,* we get *scuba*. Acronyms can be printed either in capital letters, as in NAACP, NCAA, NATO, or UNICEF, or in lowercase, as we've seen in *laser* and *scuba.*[15]

Conversion.   As the name of this type of word-formation process suggests, a conversion does not create a new word form, but it *converts* a word from one part of speech to another.[16]

There are many English words that were first used as verbs but were subsequently converted into nouns. *to walk, a walk; to laugh, a laugh; to guess, a guess.* Can you create two sentences using *butter* as both a noun and a verb? Can you do the same thing with *vacation*?

Backformation.   A specialized form of reduction, also related to conversion, a backformation will alter a noun, like *television*, for example, and create a new verb, *televise.*[17]

For some reason, this word-formation process has generated a considerable amount of controversy. Why anyone might argue with the use of a noun like *shower* undergoing a backformation to create a verb *to shower* may seem like nit-picking to you, it obviously matters to some pop grammarians. The following verbs, originally used as nouns, have been roundly criticized: *to dialogue, to parent, to interface, to impact, to host, to contact,* and *to journal.*[18] What about the noun *e-mail*? Are you hearing it used as a verb?

Converting nouns into verbs is hardly new. It's been going on for centuries. Pinker estimated, in fact, that one fifth of all English verbs were first used as nouns. Today, he said, it's common practice *to head* a committee, *foot* the bill, *toe* the line, *back* a candidate, and *shoulder* a burden.[19]

Let's consider an example from an established author. In the first paragraph of *Tender is the Night*, F. Scott Fitzgerald, certainly a recognized U.S. novelist, wrote: "Now, many bungalows cluster near it . . . ."[20] In this description of Gausse's Hotel, Fitzgerald used the verb *cluster*, a backformation of the noun, *cluster*.

Why the fuss about backformations? I don't know. If they worked for Fitzgerald, that's good enough for me. Look at it this way: I happen to like rosemary-lemon chicken; my wife doesn't. This food choice is not a question of who's right and who's wrong. As one of my favorite hosts on the TV Food Network likes to say, "Life is a matter of taste."

Be a linguist. Word origins can be fascinating information. Using your dictionary, look up the following words and explain how they came into the American English vocabulary: *bikini, jumbo, poinsettia, saxophone,* and *silhouette.*

ATTITUDES TOWARD NEW WORDS

As you can see, the English language is truly **productive**. New words can be created with relative ease. Some people see this characteristic of English as an emblem of its vigor and vitality; others see new words (or almost any change in language) as signs of mind-rot or the results of lower standards in schools.

It seems fruitless to me to reduce issues of language change to bipolar, good–bad, right–wrong choices. Language, like all other aspects of human behavior, will change, like it or not, and it doesn't necessarily mean that today's generation is lazier than previous generations or that teachers have suddenly become less demanding.

I have observed on my campus, for example, that backpack etiquette has changed. About a decade ago it was fashionable to sling one's backpack casually over one shoulder; today, the straps of the backpack are more conventionally and stylishly fitted over both shoulders. Similarly, some adolescents and young adults wear baseball-style caps indoors, sometimes with the bill in back, today. It's fashionable. It wasn't that long ago, however, that those of this same age group would never wear any kind of head covering. Some of today's clothing fashions will become tomorrow's garage-sale fodder. Some language fashions will experience a similar fate.

Times and people change. Although you and I may not fully appreciate all of the changes, our personal feelings will not stop social trends, including the formation of new words.

Nevertheless, when it comes to matters of language and how it's used, there's only one supreme court: the people who use the language.

New words will continue to be added to our vocabulary. It's inevitable, in my view, and word-watching is a fascinating activity. Stuart Berg Flexner, editor of the *Dictionary of American Slang* put it nicely, I think, when he wrote: "It is impossible for any living vocabulary to remain static."[21] Similarly, after examining changes in the English language over the span of several centuries, Aithchison observed that "language change is natural, inevitable, and continuous." Whether people consider these changes as signs of either progress or decay, Aitchison concluded that "It is in no sense wrong for human language to change."[22]

WORDS AND CULTURE

An issue related not only to the general topic of this chapter, but to the particular interests of the ENL teacher, is the special relation between a culture and the language of that culture.

For example, it is fairly common for native English speakers in some cultures to cry out "Bingo!" when they hear or observe someone say or do something especially appropriate, correct, or germane to the matters at hand. But, what will be the result if an ENL learner supplies an appropriate response to the teacher's question, and the teacher yells "Bingo!" and the learner knows not a whit about the game? Obviously, if the ENL learner comes from a culture where the game of Bingo is an unknown, "Bingo!" will have *no meaning*.

The Bingo illustration is only one example from a universe of thousands. How many times do you hear people use sports metaphors to describe everyday events in U.S. life? A court case might be described as a "slam-dunk" situation. A hopeless circumstance might be described as "fourth and long." A person who has erred has "dropped the ball." What about the individual who owes another a "major league apology?" When in doubt, do you *punt*?

Only in those cultures where people are familiar with basketball, football, and baseball, and the terminology associated with those sports, will these metaphors make any sense. My advice to ENL teachers when it comes to their using metaphors: Hold that line.

Another example of the culture–language relation can be seen in how the practices of one culture can be abhorrent to another. In the culture you and I are familiar with, a dog is often a family pet. Those of you who grew up with a pet dog will likely turn all fuzzy and warm-hearted when you recall the name of your family's pet dog. On the other hand, just try to explain to someone from the Middle East why "Rusty," "Rover," or "Blackie" claims your warm emotions. In the Middle East, a dog is a wild animal, a savage beast, never domesticated, a creature to be avoided, feared, and looked on with disgust.

Another culture-marker is a culture's mass media. In the culture I've known, the mass media have contributed a number of words and phrases to the language, although some of these contributions have had a short shelf-life.

Fifty years ago, *Fibber McGee and Molly* was a popular radio program. When Fibber McGee said something he thought was really funny, his wife, Molly, would comment: "'Taint funny,

McGee." Consequently, when people of that era heard a comment that they thought deserved a put-down, they'd say "'Taint funny, McGee."

The Life of Riley, another popular radio program in the 1940s and a popular TV program in the 1950s, featured William Bendix in the title role. Riley was the stereotypical clueless father, always getting caught between the horns of a dilemma. When he realized he was between a rock and a hard place, a no-win situation, he would usually comment, "What a revoltin' development this is." The radio-listening public appropriated this phrase and used it whenever they thought it was apt.

When *Get Smart*, starring Don Adams as a bungling spy (a spoof of the James Bond 007 popularity), was on prime-time television, Special Agent Maxwell Smart (Adams) would try to defend a seemingly outlandish claim he'd made by adding, "Would you believe … ?" This phrase became a part of society's informal discourse during the life of the TV program. When the program died the inevitable network death, so did society's use of the phrase.

More recently, McDonald's, the fast-food hamburger chain, has used the phrase "Did somebody say 'McDonald's'?" in a number of television ads. I'm hearing that phrase in informal discourse today when people adapt the McDonald's phrase to fit their circumstance, as in "Did somebody say 'golf'?' Or, "Did somebody say 'dinner'?"

The point is, a culture's mass media will often contribute to the language of that culture. By the time you read this, however, newer examples will, in all likelihood, be available. Many of these expressions are temporary.

An especially revealing example of the relation between culture and language can be drawn from an experience I had recently when another professor on my campus and I were invited to meet with visiting clergy from Russia and the Ukraine. They were in the United States in order to learn more about the relations between religion and politics, religion and governments, religion and business, and, in our case, religion and higher education.

Our setting resembled a meeting at the United Nations: Everyone sat in a circle so that we could see each other, wearing headphones so that we could hear simultaneous translations of the questions and answers.

Several times, the translators would stop either my colleague or me and comment, "We have no translatable equivalent for ____." and they'd fill in the blank. Some of the words we used that the translators couldn't find equivalents for were *peer ministry, female clergy, endowed chair,* and *hardball tactics.*

The terms Professor Whitt and I were using made sense in our culture, but these terms were unknown to our visitors who were more familiar with the Russian Orthodox tradition, Russian higher education, and Russian sports.

The moral to the story, I think, is clear: What makes common sense in one culture may be nonsense in another. Depending on their age and experience, this can be a major obstacle for your ENL students.

DICTIONARIES ARE HISTORY BOOKS

The language people use changes as they move from one region to another, from one social class to another, and from one era to another. A quality dictionary will provide a record of these changes. Contrary to some misguided popular beliefs, a dictionary is a *history* book, not a *law* book.

When a dictionary is published, it documents the entry word's pronunciation(s), part(s) of speech, and a history of the entry word's meanings, *at the time of publication.* A dictionary, then, is a book that records the history of words as they have been used up to that date.

More conservative dictionaries also employ a panel of "experts" who provide gratuitous advice regarding Do's and Don'ts about language usage. I find many of these "expert" commentaries to be elitist and arrogant; they are statements of social or political etiquette and power, not linguistic descriptions of how people actually use the language. This is my view; you'll need to decide for yourself how useful this information might be, but I hope you'll agree with me.

Have you ever thought about how a word gains entry to the dictionary? I can't provide a complete description of **lexicography**, the dictionary-making profession, but I can supply a brief overview.

Most dictionaries are based on previous publications. Members of the dictionary's editorial staff will "track" words, looking for new words (**coinages**) and new uses for existing words by reading volumes of popular and scholarly magazines, newspapers, and journals, and by listening to radio, television, and informal conversations. After collecting these observations, notations are made for any affected entry word.

The "testing ground" for many new words is the general area of slang. Flexner described **slang** as "words and expressions frequently used by or intelligible to a rather large portion of the general American public, but not accepted as good, formal usage by the majority."[23]

The ultimate decision about the social acceptance of slang, in my view, falls under the jurisdiction of the Linguistics Supreme Court: the people who use the language. Sometimes, The Court will sustain the slang usage after a trial period; sometimes, they'll render a different verdict and drop it. Through this process, **slang**, the colloquial departure from "standard" English, for one generation may become "standard" for a later generation. This is what happened with *bus*, a slang clipping of *omnibus*. At first, *bus* was judged as **slang**; today, it's standard. The same thing happened with *zoo*, from *zoological* garden and *piano*, from *pianoforte*.[24]

Some examples of current slang are *dead presidents* (money, since U.S. currency features pictures of former presidents); *head-banger* (either a performer or a fan of heavy metal music); *gender-bender* (a person who either looks or acts like a member of the opposite sex); and *smash-mouth* (rough, aggressive football). By the time you read this book, all of these slang expressions may have been dispensed with by the People's Supreme Court. Conversely, one or more of them may have been sustained for general usage. So it goes with slang.

THE USE(S) OF THE DICTIONARY

Often, people will encounter a usage whose validity they question and they'll look up the word or phrase in their dictionary in order to determine whether the utterance is "acceptable," "approved," "nonstandard," or whatever. After locating the usage in question, some people will then pronounce a judgment based on what they have read in The Dictionary (note the capital letters). The use of the definite article in this case is misleading. It suggests that there's *one* dictionary containing all the information about words anyone might want to know. This simply is not the case.

A casual stroll through your favorite bookstore will reveal an inescapable fact: There are many editions of American English dictionaries, each published in accord with different editorial policies determining how entry words are selected for inclusion, the representation of alternate spellings, the presentation (or not) of **etymologies** (word histories), and whether some definitions, pronunciations, and the like, will be labeled "nonstandard," "standard," "colloquial," "dialect," and so on.

Book publishing is an expensive, highly competitive business. Consequently, the dictionaries produced by different publishers will vary, each following different policies with regard to how prescriptive or descriptive their dictionary will be. Among the book-buying public there are those who want to be told how the language *must* be used, and there are those who want to know how the language *has* been used. There's a dictionary available for those at either end of this spectrum, although I prefer the descriptive text, for reasons I have already explained.

Given the differing stances dictionary publishers adopt, my advice is to look up a questionable spelling, definition, or pronunciation in at least two dictionaries!

For example, both in high school and during my undergraduate studies , there was one and only one spelling for the word *judgmental*. (And I just did it.) I invite you to consult the most current collegiate dictionaries available to you in order to determine the spelling of this word. I suspect you'll find *two* conventional spellings for this word today. What does this tell you about spelling instruction in ENL classes?

Although not all dictionaries contain identical data describing words, there are certain commonalties among most reputable dictionaries.

Except for *pictionaries* produced for the primary grades, most American English dictionaries will contain the following:

1. Main entry words (head words, entry words), called **lemmata** by lexicographers. The words are printed in bold face, in alphabetical order. Information provided for each main entry word typically includes the word's conventional spelling and any recognized alternative spellings, when appropriate. For example, some dictionaries will include both *center* and *centre, meager* and *meagre* as conventional spellings for these words, although the very conservative spell-checker on my word processing program does not. Be advised that spell-checkers are not always current.

Organizing words in a dictionary by alphabetical order makes all kinds of sense, given the history of dictionaries (or the needs of the anal-retentive), but it makes no sense at all for those who are interested in the semantic, or meaning, relationships among words. In any dictionary you care to consult, for example, you'll find the words *animal, bear, cat, dog, elephant, fish, guinea pig, hamster,* etc., etc., etc., all the way to *zebra,* in different sections of the dictionary, which is organized in alphabetical order, remember. A book advertised as a **lexicon** (rather than a dictionary) of the English language will list related words accordingly. A lexicon therefore, may be more useful to the ENL learner.

2. Pronunciation suggestions and alternatives will be provided, typically using an augmented form of the International Phonetic Alphabet in the respellings. The phonetic respellings usually include the most frequently occurring pronunciation of the entry word, but will also include recognized and equally acceptable pronunciations used in different geographic regions.

One of the greatest injustices promulgated in the dimly lit past is the notion that the first pronunciation is the *preferred,* or better, pronunciation. That simply isn't true.

3. The **etymology,** or the history of the word, will be given. In some dictionaries, the etymology is near the beginning of the entry, whereas other dictionaries may include it toward the end. The location of the etymology isn't as important as *whether* an etymology is given. The etymology provides the "family tree" for the entry word, describing the other language(s) from which the entry word was derived.

4. For each entry word, several definitions, or **senses**, will be given. For many ENL learners this is obviously important information, and you'll need to provide direct instruction to them, in my view, in order to demonstrate how they can select the most appropriate definition, given the word's context in a sentence. Another dictionary myth is "the first definition is the preferred definition." This a patently false. Look up the word *watch* in your dictionary and explain to someone how the first definition listed is inherently preferred over the others.

5. Some dictionaries will also include **labels of convenience**, sometimes referred to as **usage notes**, indicating whether a particular pronunciation or definition is, in the judgment of the editorial staff, *archaic, obsolete, slang,* or a *dialect* feature.[25]

This list includes only the most basic types of information most dictionaries will provide about each word. Some will provide additional data, including the actual date the word first appeared in print; cross references to synonyms and antonyms; homographs; parts of speech, and the like. One of the collegiate dictionaries in my study provides 46 separate explanatory notes for main entry words.

At the other end of the spectrum, you'll be able to find inexpensive paperback dictionaries providing very little of the information described here. These dictionaries usually provide only one spelling, one pronunciation, and only one or two definitions. Because the information in these dictionaries is so limited, they have no value in a classroom, in my judgment, neither for native English speakers, nor, especially, those students for whom English is a new language

Publishers have recently addressed the needs of ENL learners and have begun to publish English language dictionaries especially for them. The ones I've seen are very attractive, they include many more illustrations in an entry, and they include several sentences in each entry showing a word's possible uses.

The collegiate desk dictionary is the U.S. contribution to the science of dictionary-making. These one-volume dictionaries are especially attractive, I think, because they are relatively inexpensive, up to date, and portable.

Consider that unabridged dictionaries—those large tomes resting on dictionary stands—are revised on a 25- to 30-year cycle and collegiate dictionaries are revised on a 10-year cycle. The collegiate dictionary will, obviously, be able to reflect more recent additions to the English vocabulary and newer uses of words in a timely manner.

How words enter the language and how these processes are recorded in dictionaries is fascinating information. The learning of words, their definitions, pronunciations, and spellings is a major challenge for the ENL learner. Enabling the ENL learner to name things and ideas is of the most altruistic and humanizing endeavors you will ever experience.

FOR DISCUSSION

Part 1. Place a ✓ beside each statement found in the chapter.

___ 1. Ultimately, the first definition in a dictionary is more accurate.
___ 2. When people need a new word, they'll create one.
___ 3. The earlier, older, definition is usually more accurate.
___ 4. Nouns can be used as adjectives, but not as verbs.
___ 5. People change faster than do dictionaries.

Part 2. Place a ✓ beside each statement the text would support.

___ 6. Word-formation processes illustrate the principle of productivity.
___ 7. *Language* and *culture* are two names for the same concept.
___ 8. People use language their peers will approve of.
___ 9. Linguistic symbols are universal.
___ 10. Any dictionary is obsolete.

Part 3. Based on what you know and what you have read in this chapter, place a ✓ beside each statement with which you can agree.

___ 11. Utility usually takes precedence over purism.

___ 12. Fashion determines acceptance.

___ 13. Behavior informs observation.

___ 14. When it doubt, simplify.

___ 15. *Everybody's doing it* is no explanation for one's behavior.

NOTES

1. Jean Nienkamp (ed.), *Plato on Rhetoric and Language* (Mahwah, NJ: Lawrence Erlbaum Associates, 1999), 6–7.
2. Ibid.
3. *Merriam Webster's Collegiate Dictionary* (10th ed., Spring-field, MA: Merriam-Webster, 1993), 886.
4. "Wired World Creates New Words," *Lincoln* (NE) Journal Star, August 24, 1999, A-4.
5. Fred West, *The Way of Language* (New York: Harcourt Brace, 1975), 4.
6. George Yule, *The Study of Language* (Cambridge, England: Cambridge University Press, 1985), 1.
7. *The Holy Qur'an*, S.xxx.22.
8. *Merriam Webster's Collegiate Dictionary*, 566.
9. Ibid., 504.
10. Robert Hendrickson, *American Talk: The Words and Ways of American Dialects* (New York: Penguin Books, 1987), 25.
11. Ibid., 25–27.
12. Ibid., 51–52.
13. Adrian Akmajian, Richard D. Demers, Ann K. Farmer, and Robert M. Harnish, *Linguistics: An Introduction to Language and Communication* (3rd ed., Cambridge, MA: MIT Press, 1990), 24.
14. Albert C. Baugh and Thomas Cable, *A History of the English Language* (3rd ed., Englewood Cliffs, NJ: Prentice-Hall), 257.
15. Yule, 53.
16. Jeffrey Kaplan, *English Grammar: Principles and Facts* (Englewood Cliffs, NJ: Prentice-Hall, 1989), 36.
17. Akmajian et al., 14.
18. Steven Pinker, *The Language Instinct* (New York: Morrow, 1994), 8.
19. Ibid.
20. F. Scott Fitzgerald, *Tender is the Night* (New York: Charles Scribner's Sons, 1933), 1.

21. Stuart Berg Flexner, "'Preface' to the *Dictionary of American Slang*," in Paul Escholz et al. (Eds.), *Language Awareness* (4th ed., New York: St. Martin's Press, 1986), 182.
22. Jean Aitchison, *Language Change: Progress or Decay?* (New York: Universe Books, 1981), 222.
23. Flexner, 180.
24. David Crystal (ed.), *The Cambridge Encyclopedia of Language* (2nd ed., Cambridge, England: Cambridge University Press, 1997), 53.
25. Robert Burchfield, "The Oxford English Dictionary," in Robert Illson (ed.), *Lexicography: An Emerging Profession* (Manchester, England: Manchester University Press, 1986), 19.

CHAPTER 3

English Use and Usage

"Sick have I become."
"Strong am I with the force."
"Your father he is."

—Yoda, *The Empire Strikes Back*

As you approach this chapter, imagine the following scenario: A colleague approaches you in the staff lounge. "Say," the colleague begins, "I don't want to complain, but how long will it take your ESL kids to learn the difference between 'lie' and 'lay' or 'between you and I' and 'between you and me?' Don't you people explain what proper grammar is?" How many replies are there to this colleague?

LANGUAGE AND EXPECTATIONS

Yoda, the Jedi Master quoted here uses a word order that native English speakers can recognize but do not often employ. In the film *The Empire Strikes Back*, Yoda's speech and word order help to create an atmosphere of mystery, intrigue, and wonder. Viewers accept this almost poetical style of language because it contributes significantly to Yoda's character and the ambiance of the film. On the other hand, if an ENL learner in your school were to speak this same way, many would, no doubt, shake their heads and mutter, "Tsk, tsk tsk."

Beyond the theater walls, Yoda's sentence structure may sound just a bit too foreign. The sentences aren't what we generally expect or anticipate.

Perhaps the most frequent word order in a sentence either spoken or written by a native English speaker is the subject–verb–object (S–V–O) pattern that we see in the sentences *Sally arrived yesterday* and *Larry works diligently*. Occasionally, we might hear an O–V–S pattern, as in *Linda I called, not Tim*. Rarely do we expect an encounter with the O–S–V pattern seen in Yoda's comments, which is probably why it was used in the film.

It is clearly beyond the scope of a single chapter to present a complete grammar of American English for the ENL teacher. There are many good grammar texts available for a more detailed discussion.

Although this book is neither a grammar text nor an ENL teaching methods text, there are some suggestions I offer about the role of grammar instruction in the ENL program.

For starters, think about this: If you enjoy spirited discussions, approach a group of people at the next party you attend and ask them "Are you people pro-choice or pro-life?" If this question doesn't create a response, try "What should the schools teach, creationism or evolution?" Or, especially if there are school teachers or school patrons in the crowd, you might try "Should we teach grammar in the schools?"

I suspect any one of these questions will provide the discussion you're looking for.

Although I do not have any special knowledge to offer you regarding the first two questions, I can report to you that I have heard many debates, indeed, I've participated in some, with regard to the third question!

Some people, professional educators as well as lay persons, believe that the teaching of grammar is the center, the galvanizing core of any language-learning curriculum. Others, professional educators and lay persons, believe that grammar is too abstract, too confusing, too hard, and too removed from the realities of everyday communication for it to receive much attention in schools.

Before we tackle those issues, let's clarify some terms so that we are at least singing out of the same songbook.

For most linguists, grammar is divided into phonology, syntax, and semantics. **Phonology** is the study of the sounds used in a language; **syntax** is the study of how words in a sentence relate to each other in ways acceptable to and understood by the native speakers of that language; **semantics** is the study of meanings, signification, and how the words, meanings, and people interact.

Crystal has described different types of grammar. A **descriptive grammar** describes the ways language is used without making judgments about the social acceptability of any of the uses. A **pedagogical grammar** is usually found in the grammar textbooks used in schools. A **prescriptive grammar**, also often used in schools, is typically a book or a manual and it presents lists of *do use* versus *don't use* rules, or prescriptions. A reference grammar is a large compendium describing how a language is systematically organized.[1]

Crystal's descriptions help to illustrate just how complex the notion of *grammar* can be for you in your role as an ENL teacher. Although it is important for you to determine which grammar is informing your teaching, or which grammar you are referring to when you use the word *grammar*, there are some important pedagogical matters to be examined.

To illustrate, please join me while we visit a class taught by Nancy Ford, a former graduate student of mine and an outstanding language educator who used to teach in the Intensive English Program (IEP) on our campus. The IEP program is offered for those undergraduate and graduate students whose Test of English as a Foreign Language (TOEFL) scores indicate that additional instruction in English will likely enhance their chances for academic success at the university.

Nancy would typically bring many different examples of authentic English language uses to her classroom: a videotape of a TV talk show, news program, or commercial; or, an article or two from the morning newspaper; or, articles from different types of popular magazines. She and her students would view the videotapes or read the articles, then discuss—in English, of course—the topics addressed. Sometimes they might debate the issues found in the tapes or articles. They would write personal responses in their journals to the reading or viewing activities, connecting their understandings with what they had been studying in the textbook. They would read their reflections aloud, and discuss them.

Her classes were very interactive; students were reading, writing, talking, and reflecting in meaningful ways. They were learning and helping each other to learn English.

Toward the end of a class session, however, a student would inevitably remark, "Nancy, this is fun, but when are we going to study English?"

I know enough about Nancy's classes to understand the students' comments. They wanted to know when they were going to receive a worksheet giving them opportunities to practice identifying parts of speech, and the like. Nancy's class didn't meet their expectations. But, they also didn't understand that they had been "doing" English for almost an hour.

Granted, Nancy's students are older than the K–12 students you may be teaching or intend to teach, but the illustration from Nancy's classroom can still be generalized to the K–12 curriculum in this way: When you are teaching about the structure of English, you must distinguish, in my view, between English *use* and English *usage*.

USE VERSUS USAGE

When students try to learn a new language, they want to be able to *communicate* in that language as soon as possible. For too many years, however, we have approached second language and learning and teaching based on an assumption that the learners must first learn the forms and functions of the new language *before* they can communicate in and through it.[2]

Consequently, many language curricula emphasize the presentation of language forms and accompanying nomenclature, devoid of meaningful contexts. These programs emphasize grammatical competence (**usage**) rather than communicative competence (**use**).

Henry Widdowson has been my teacher more often than he'll ever know. He helped me understand the distinction between **usage** and **use**. Widdowson described how a student might learn how to identify or how to create an S–V–O English sentence, such as *I like popcorn*. This is an idealized English sentence, and it's grammatical. The student who can produce a sentence like this has demonstrated grammatical competence (**usage**). Examined out of context, no one familiar with English grammar would question whether *I like popcorn* is a well-formed sentence.

*Popcorn like I or **Like popcorn I*, on the other hand, are clearly not grammatical, and would not demonstrate usage competence.[3] (Asterisks placed before constructions in language texts conventionally denote an unlikely expression.)

By way of contrast, if you ask one of your ENL students, *What's your address?*, it makes no difference at all whether the student replies *I like popcorn* or *Popcorn like I*, because neither answer demonstrates correct **use** of the language. Both replies to the question are equally wrong, in the communicative (**use**) sense, despite the fact that one of them is grammatically acceptable (**usage**).[4]

The general weakness of many grammar drills and worksheets is that although they may help the ENL learner to gain competence in English **usage**, they too often do little to help the student gain competence in learning how to **use** the language for meaningful and authentic purposes.

I might add at this point that one of the recurring weaknesses, in my judgment, in some of the ENL research reported in professional journals describing which type(s) of instructional strategies and interventions may be more or less effective is the failure to distinguish between English **usage** and English **use**.

A final illustration may help to make my point about **usage** and **use**. More years ago than I care to remember, I enrolled in a first-year Spanish course in high school. Throughout the first quarter of that school year we studied Spanish nouns, verbs, adjectives, and so on. During the first 14 weeks of the school year, I think I completed well over 200 worksheet activities in which I examined the grammatical nuances of *ser* and *estar*; I could conjugate *–er* and *–ir* verbs, including the irregulars; I learned *azul, blanco, verde*, and the other names in the rainbow.

The first sentence I ever generated all by myself in my Spanish I class was *I have a green pencil box*. The teacher was proud of me. However, some 40 years later, I am still waiting for an opportunity to use that sentence in *authentic* social discourse. My sentence was grammatical and it demonstrated Spanish **usage** competence, but it served no communicative purpose.

To extend this discussion one more centimeter, recall my description in chapter 1 of my trip to Bolivia to visit my younger daughter. She had meetings all of one afternoon, so I remained in her apartment to read some of the materials I had taken with me in my briefcase. The telephone rang and I answered it. *¿Está Sally?*, the caller asked ("Is Sally there?"). After I replied, *No* (What a conversationalist!), I was reduced to total inarticulacy in the **use** of Spanish. I studied Spanish **usage** for 5 years!

What does all of this mean for you, an ENL teacher? I think it means this, as Larsen-Freeman described it:

> It is for students to simply have knowledge insufficient of target language forms, meanings, and functions. Students must be able to apply this knowledge in negotiating meaning. It is through the interaction between speaker and listener (or reader and writer) that meaning becomes clear. The listener gives the speaker feedback as to whether she understands what the speaker has said. In this way, the speaker can revise what he has said and try to communicate the meaning again.[5]

Be a linguist. A good dose of grammar instruction, some believe, is as effective as a good dose of castor oil in the purging of irregularities. Explain how grammar instruction might improve these sentences:

1. Females dominate conversations.
2. St. Louis is east of New York.
3. The chicken was too hot to eat.
4. Everyone should bring his money tomorrow.
5. She gave the dog it's food..

RESPONDING TO ERRORS

In Nancy's classes, the students will write or speak unconventional or unlikely constructions. This happens in every ENL class I have seen; it also routinely happens in classes filled with native English speakers. The unconventional expressions seem to loom larger in the eyes of some, however, in the ENL class. Some ENL teachers become more concerned than I believe they should when they detect production errors and are compelled to correct every miscue. On the other hand, there are some ENL teachers who ignore every miscue.

My advice is this: Resist the temptation to correct every error, spoken or written. Furthermore, especially with older ENL learners, resist also their requests for you to correct them whenever they make an error.

Instead, I recommend two basic strategies. First, always provide for your students, in your writing and speaking, the most appropriate model of use that is most commonly used in your community. Second, provide direct instruction and corrective feedback with those items carrying the greatest social stigma in society.

For example, I wouldn't allocate a great deal of time and energy, other things being equal, to devise activities to help your students distinguish between (1) *He gave the book to Tom and me* versus (2) *He gave the book to Tom and I*. Although Sentence 2 may irritate your ears, I submit that fully 50% of the native English-speaking public can't make the distinction. For better or worse, there's little social stigma attached to the confusion between the objective and subjective first-person pronouns. I hear *I* and *me* used interchangeably today in the objective position, largely because of hypercorrection.

You and I may not like this emergent change in American English grammar, but it happens with increasing regularity. Remember, that our job is *not* to prepare ENL learners in our image, but in concert with the English-speaking culture they will live in.

On the other hand, if the *I* and *me* distinction is important to you, *model* the appropriate use, but don't make it a bigger deal than it is.

Conversely, if you read or hear *He given the book to Tom and me*, I would discretely attend to that error right away. This construction will be stigmatized.

Everything I've just said will not be unanimously supported in the ENL teaching community. I am basing my suggestions on classroom practicalities and sociolinguistic realities, as I see them. Although I hope you will agree with me, I promise I will never visit your classroom as an uninvited observer to determine whether you're Doing the Right Things.

USE YOUR LINGUISTIC EXPERIENCES

Richard Hudson observed that most of the language instruction you and I received in our earlier school days had at least two characteristics:

1. It stressed the things we did *not* know about language.
2. It implied that there is only one standard of correctness.

I can't speak for you, of course, but when I began my junior high schooling (long before the days of middle schools), I was astonished to learn how little I knew about the language I had been speaking, reading, and writing all my life. My seventh-grade English teacher prepared what I remember as the most diabolical grammar worksheets imaginable. I became convinced that the Andrews family was a motley collection of mental and social outcasts, doomed to the lowest levels of linguistic corruption and squalor. With the onset of the seventh grade my language was discredited and disavowed.

I learned that ending sentences with prepositions was an activity only idiots and morons participated in. I learned that splitting infinitives was something to always avoid. Before the seventh grade, I never knew these things.

What I know today is that these two features of traditional classroom grammar rules—do not end sentences with prepositions and do not split infinitives—are rules describing how *other* languages might work, but not English. These two rules accurately describe Latin and other Romance languages, but they don't describe English syntax.

In Latin, for example, the parts of speech we call *prepositions* cannot be placed at the end of a sentence (which is why they're called *prepositions*, not *postpositions*). If these words appear at the end of a Latin sentence, the sentence isn't grammatical. Ovid would have put an asterisk at the head of such a sentence. In English, however, it is physically possible to put a preposition at the end of a sentence. If doing so violates a rule, it's somebody's *social* rule, not a descriptive grammar rule.

Similarly, the same generalization holds for the *split infinitive* rule. In Romance languages the infinitive verb form appears as a single unit, one word. For example, the Latin infinitive verb *dictare* is roughly equivalent to the English infinitive verb *to dictate*. Although *dictare* cannot be divided with an interposed word, the English equivalent can be divided, as in *to cruelly dictate*. The same can be said about the Latin infinitive *efficere*, roughly equivalent to the English *to bring about*, or *to effect*. Although *efficere* cannot be divided or split, the English equivalent can, as in *to finally effect closure*.

In Spanish, the infinitive *leer* is one word, equivalent to the English infinitive *to read*. Although *leer* cannot be divided or split, the English equivalent can be divided, split, as in *to carefully read, to carelessly read,* or *to blindly read*.

What all of this means to you as a teacher of ENL learners is, in my view, relatively simple: Do not rely on traditional rules of **pedagogical** or **prescriptive** grammars. These grammars simply do not always describe how the English language is organized. They may be statements describing social etiquette or political correctness, but they aren't valid grammatical descriptions.

Furthermore, taking a grammar rule from one language and trying to force it onto another language is similar to jamming an audiotape into a compact disc player. It won't play, in Peoria or anywhere else.

The belief in a single standard of correctness is similarly flawed. As ENL learners grow in their English language proficiency, many of them will ask you, "Is this [English construction] correct?" What they're asking for, as some native English speaker-writers ask for, is a codified list of correct uses of English.

When your ENL learners ask this question, you must, first of all, make a distinction between *spoken* and *written* uses of English (*uses* here in the manner Widdowson described them). As you intuitively know, English speakers accept greater variation in spoken language than they do written language.

In spoken English, for example, one might say *Norman, I ain't taking this foolishness from these here fish no more!* I actually used this sentence, as best I can remember, with my next door neighbor; he and I go fishing whenever the weather is cooperative. Norman accepted this sentence as a lame alibi for why we weren't catching any fish; he knew I was mangling the language, trying to interject some humor in an otherwise humorless circumstance. A construction similar to this sentence, however, would not be acceptable in other, more formal, contexts.

The standards for oral and written English are different. You use more casual language in conversation than you do in most written language. Use your examined language experiences as your guide as you help ENL learners distinguish between the two sets of standards.

STANDARD ENGLISH

Speaking of standards, *Standard English* is a term widely discussed in the ENL teaching community throughout the world. Standard English is not only discussed in this chapter, but again in chapter 5 in consideration of U.S. dialects.

We can approach Standard English from at least two perspectives. First, what is Standard English as it may affect ENL programs; and, second, what is *Standard English* in your classroom teaching philosophy and repertoire?

Because Great Britain has a much older tradition of teaching English as another language than does the United States, much of the current discussion about how to define *Standard English* emanates from language scholars in Great Britain and may, therefore, seem unrelated to the needs of teachers in the United States. In the long run, in my view, it's not unrelated to our concerns; we're simply entering the conversation a bit late.

For European educational purposes, Standard English has been considered by many to be British English (BrE), not American English (AmE). Most of the language-learning scholars in Great Britain, however, view *Standard English* as being represented by both varieties, BrE as well as AmE.[7]

The debate concerning whether to use either BrE or AmE as *the standard* for English language proficiency is much more widespread in Great Britain and Europe than it is in the United States. Why? I suspect that there are more AmE speakers and writers in the world. Nevertheless, as the ENL enterprise continues to become a global endeavor, this debate will reach greater heights of vigorous discussion, in my view. This issue is especially important if you're planning to teach ENL abroad. Which flavor of English, BrE or AmE, will be the standard where you will teach? You need to know this at the beginning.

U.S. STANDARDS

Given the recent national attention to the establishment of K–12 standards for learning attainments in U.S. schools, you will, no doubt, have an opportunity to create benchmarks for the English language proficiency of your ENL students. Remember that Standard English is a composite of language attributes that are used by successful speakers of the language, and is not a prescriptive model, patterned after the privileged native English speakers of a prestige variety.[8]

Your experiences with English have already helped you to distinguish some of the ways speakers from different regions of the United States pronounce words differently. Nevertheless, despite those regional variations, one particular variety, *Standard American English* (SAE), is often named by people as the national standard for correct use.

SAE is an idealized concept and not a fixed code. Furthermore, what is acceptable as SAE in conversations in Atlanta,

Georgia, will vary from what is acceptable SAE in South Boston, Manhattan, New York, or Manhattan, Kansas.

You may have heard people in your social circles or at school refer to SAE as if it were a list of sanctioned usages. Those who refer to SAE assume they know what they're talking about and they assume others know, too.

This may not, however, be the case, my pastor, the Rev. Dr. Ra Drake, frequently refers to the *membuhs* of her congregation. I call them *members*. The difference is not caused by her ordination, or the lack of mine, but by her background, as well as mine. In my native dialect, the final /r/ is typically pronounced; in her native dialect, the final /r/ is often dropped. She was raised in the U.S. Southern Dialect region; I in the Midwest region. I contend we both speak SAE.

Similarly, I grew up describing some foods as *greazy*. Both of my daughters, products of the same gene pool, were raised in the Upper North Midland dialect area. They render the word *greasy*. Again, I think we're all speaking SAE.

In addition to these pronunciation differences within the broad category called SAE, there are additional variations.

For example, at the university where I attended graduate school, the word *data* was always a plural noun, as in *The data are inconclusive*. Those graduate students who used *data* as a singular noun were corrected.

Today, however, I'm reading and hearing *data* used either as often or more often as a singular noun. One of my collegiate dictionaries reflects this trend with the usage note, "sing or pl in constr." Remember, most dictionaries try to record how the language is used, not how it ought to be used. Clearly, the oral and written uses of *data* are changing, but both reflect SAE, I believe.

Please understand that I am not suggesting that you disregard calling attention to language conventions our society will expect your students to observe. That would be unprofessional and irresponsible. Rather, I hope that you will help your students, depending on their age and English proficiency, to distinguish the different communication requirements they face in oral and written English, and to help them understand that more than one choice can sometimes be correct.

WHAT IS "GOOD ENGLISH"

I receive questions all the time about the English language and how people ought to use it. This is a strange circumstance, because the question assumes that people were made for language, and not the other way around. The questions come at me in my office, at the supermarket, over the backyard fence, at church, and over the telephone and e-mail lines. However the questions are phrased, they are all asking, in one form or another, *What is Good English?*

Sampson believes this question is especially important in the United States. Those who use American English may lack linguistic self-confidence, he says, possibly because of the large number of speaker/writers whose command of American English is only one or two generations old.[9]

Carlson, on the other hand, described what he considered long-lived fears in the United States of almost any form of human difference. This fear has resulted, Carlson suggested, in a national crusade for homogeneity, for sameness, for conformity, for doctrinal orthodoxy, especially in those areas that are most visible: like habits, personal appearance, and language.[10]

Whether you agree or disagree with either Sampson or Carlson, you can no doubt recognize the *What is Good English?* question. Perhaps you've asked it. However the question is framed, it seems to assume that there's a list of Good English Usages some people (like me?) have memorized. I know of no such list.

The definition of **Good English** I use, not nearly as simple as it appears on the surface, was first offered by Pooley:

> "Good English" is marked by success in making language choices so that the fewest number of participants will be distracted by the choices.[11]

Pooley's definition avoids a familiar word, the word *ungrammatical*. As Bulley pointed out, the word *ungrammatical* implies "wrong," but in what sense? Clearly not a moral sense, although some who use the label *ungrammatical* sometimes try to invoke a notion of morality against those who speak differently.[12] Instead, Pooley pointed us in the direction of both sanity and reality.

Pooley's definition, in my view, includes the following:

"Good English" is Appropriate to the Speaker or Writer's Purpose.[13] Throughout a given space of time, we will find ourselves in communications contexts that range from the very formal to the very informal and casual. Along this continuum, our purposes for communicating vary to fit the context. Users of **Good English** know that there are differences between a lecture and a casual conversation. Whether you are chatting with a friend about her daughter's college plans, or addressing a local civic organization about a school bond issue that will be voted on the following week, you are able to shift, almost unconsciously, your language style to fit the context. After all, you don't want your friend to think you've turned uppity and you don't want the civic organization to think you are an unschooled clod.

People who consistently use only one language style, either overly formal or downright casual, regardless of their purpose, are likely to be viewed as pedantic boors or capricious clowns. Either case is distracting and results in "Bad English."

"Good English" is Appropriate to the Context.[14] If a teacher meets with the Program Committee of the building's Parent–Teacher Organization after school and talks to the committee members using the same language he used with his first graders earlier in the day, the contextual expectations have been violated. This is an *adult* business meeting, for Pete's sake.

This example may sound far-fetched, but I once taught with an individual who always referred to herself in faculty meetings the same way she referred to herself in her primary level classroom. You can imagine how the rest us responded when she'd say something like "Mrs. Blank thinks the new schedule is just fine." She was serious! Her language use was distracting and did not fit the context. It's another example of "Bad English."

"Good English" is Comfortable Both to the Speaker and the Listener.[15] Imagine you are greeting parents in your classroom for "Back to School Night" or some other type of open house, and you couch your remarks in highly technical vocabulary that is familiar only to you and your teacher colleagues; some parents feel uncomfortable or distracted, or both. Some may not understand what you're saying and some may become upset because they think you're either showing off, or that you're not a good communicator with their children, either. Any benefits the school may have realized from the open house are gone.

This definition of **Good English** will correspond, I suspect, to what you've already observed, perhaps intuitively, about some language events you've experienced. It may very well be that all I've done here is to give you some labels for your intuitions.

Earlier, I mentioned the use of highly technical vocabulary. Clearly, there are times when these word choices will be appropriate, just as there are times when they won't be. Similarly, there are times when the use of a male pronoun might be appropriate, and then there are times when it isn't, and the language sounds sexist.

I understand that there are those who may disagree with my examples of technical vocabulary or sexist language. Someone might say, "I'm a professional educator and I intend to talk like one." Or, "This sexist language thing has been blown out of proportion; male pronouns don't bother me."

These examples, and others like them, may, however, be bothersome to others. **Good English**, as we're defining it here, is *other-oriented*. Look at it this way, if you're having friends over for dinner and you know one of your friends is allergic to shrimp, will you prepare the shrimp anyway? The language user who chooses to ignore or to violate the features in our definition is certainly free to do so, but this person must also be prepared to accept the consequences.

> *Be a linguist.* You may need your dictionary for this activity. Explain how the following may or may not be con-

sidered Standard or Nonstandard English:
1. I'm *agin* it.
2. Do you feel *alright*?
3. Jim *busted* his wristwatch.
4 *Irregardless*, I'm going.
5. *Ain't* he a piece of work?

If the participants in a language exchange become distracted, communication will suffer. They may pay more attention to *how* something is being said rather than *what* is being said. Taken to what I believe is a logical conclusion, if the participants become distracted by poor choices by the writer or speaker, they may discredit him or her as arrogant, rude, unreliable, or plain stupid. These judgments may not be correct, but they represent a serious **social tax** society levied against those whose English use creates discomfort or distraction.

Societies usually assess social taxes against those who violate cultural norms and expectations. If an adult dinner guest eats green beans with his fingers, it'll be a long time, I'll bet, before you ask him back. Eating habits, wardrobe choices, and language use represent only three areas of human behavior that are governed, I suggest, by our definition of **Good English**.

SOME CLASSROOM IMPLICATIONS

A student's question about the appropriateness of a particular item of language use can seldom be answered with a simple *right* or *wrong* reply from the teacher. The teacher's life would certainly be simpler if this were the case, but, as I hope you've seen, language use is so intertwined with its context that the standard of **Good English** is a floating concept.

In one of my language courses, the students and I have laughed with each other several times when we've realized that the vast majority of the questions we ask each other about English in **use** can be answered, at least initially, with "What's the context?"

Those who are engaged in the Search for Language Certainty will be very uncomfortable with this notion. One of my best friends has been afflicted with this search for as long as I've known him. One time he declared, "Dr. Andrews (whenever he uses my title, I know what follows will be a question about language usage), surely you'd mark it as 'wrong' if one of your students used, 'Youse guys' in a paper turned in to you for course credit."

"Well," I replied, "that depends."

"'Depends,' Hell!" He went on: "Dr. Andrews, you know that 'Youse guys' is *never* acceptable in written English!"

I have a number of possible comments I could offer here in defense of my "that depends" reply, but I'll hold them. In your judgment, when might *Youse guys* be considered appropriate language use, or "Good English?"

The English language worksheet or handbook approach to grammar or usage study is used by a number of teachers, in both ENL and English classes. On these pages students are confronted with a series of sentences that are presented in a decontextualized list:

Alright, I'm ready for a Scrabble match.

Put that trunk anywhere that it will fit.

Aren't you interested in this drawing, Stan?[16]

The students are supposed to circle and then correct what's wrong in each sentence, or they are supposed to write another "correct" sentence following the model provided. You've seen these types of activities, I'll wager.

I don't know about you, but I do not know *one* person in all of the groups in which I am a member who walks around creating single-sentence, one-shot observations about the universe of potential events. Most people use language in connected, interactive, and responsive ways, with real purposes in mind in actual social contexts. As the contexts change, and as the participants change (consider here also our social and political relationships with the participants), we are left, I submit, with the inevitable conclusion that what constitutes "Good English" **must** be considered on a case-by-case basis.

I am not suggesting that "anything is acceptable as long as communication takes place." I've heard that tired bromide before and I reject it.

What I am stating is this: The issues of "Good English" must be considered honestly and the conclusion will be determined by using multiple criteria, not a single standard, of what is "correct."

If you think about it for just a moment, you'll recognize the fact that we use multiple criteria for "what's right" in other parts of our lives. If you're shopping for a pair of shoes, for example, you've probably given thought to what kind of shoes you're looking for: Casual or formal? To wear when teaching, playing golf, or when attending a fancy (or not fancy) social event? What matters more, style, appearance, color, or comfort?

ENL learners, especially those who are either older or more advanced in their English-language proficiency, need to understand that judgments about English-language use will be determined by society as either "Good English" or "Bad English" to the extent that they can analyze and explain the following: **Who is saying what to whom for what purpose under which circumstances?**

The "who" part of the question causes us to consider the social, political, academic, economic, interracial, male–female, and so on, relationships between or among the participants, all of which are important factors when we decide what "Good English" is. The "what" refers either to the topic or to the formulaic usage employed. "To whom" refers again to the complicated relationships already described. "For what purposes" recognizes that we may want to inform, to clarify, to offer friendly interactional comments, and the like. Similarly, "under which circumstances" addresses the concept of context of use. Whether the circumstance is a family reunion, testimony in a court of law, a telephone call to a brother or sister, the late-night news broadcast, a special mailing describing a sale at a local hardware store, or a newspaper editorial, the context of use will affect the use of language.

"Who is saying what to whom for what purposes under which circumstances?" is a thorough analysis for language-use questions. Granted, it's more difficult than completing handbook pages, but it's a more valid approach to language study.

As you provide your students with diverse reading, speaking, or writing activities, as you bring your classes audio- and videotapes of radio and television language use examples, and as you bring to your classes examples of language use found in newspapers (including advertisement supplements), magazines, billboards, menus, junk mail, and the like, and as you and your students discuss **Who is saying what to whom for what purposes under which circumstance**, they will become better observers of the social requirements for "Good English."

FOR DISCUSSION

Directions. Based on what you know and what you have read in this chapter, how will you answer the following questions?

1. Where do you place the teaching of American English grammar in your curriculum: at the center or on the edge? Somewhere else?
2. What do you think ENL learners need first, knowledge of the *forms* of English or the *uses* of English? Why do you believe this?
3. What are the differences between language *usage* and language *use*, in your own words?
4. Like native English speakers, ENL students will make errors. Which ones will you attend to, and why?
5. Are standards of achievement negotiable under certain circumstances?
6. Why are the conventions shaping written and spoken English different?
7. Which language errors are more serious to you: factual, social, or grammatical?
8. In your own words, what constitutes "Bad English?"
9. In language discussions, why is the word *context* so important, and so often ignored by the general public?
10. How are the concepts of *culture* and *context* related?

NOTES

1. David Crystal, *The Cambridge Encyclopedia of Language* (2nd ed., Cambridge, England: Cambridge University Press, 1997), 88.
2. Yvonne S. Freeman and David E. Freeman, *ENL/EFL Teaching: Principles for Success* (Portsmouth, NH: Heinemann, 1998), 154.
3. Henry Widdowson, *Teaching Language as Communication* (Oxford, England: Oxford University Press, 1978), 233.
4. Ibid.
5. Diane Larsen-Freeman, *Techniques and Principles of Language Teaching* (Oxford, England: Oxford University Press, 1986), 123.
6. Richard Hudson, *Invitation to Linguistics* (Oxford, England: Oxford University Press, 1986), 38.
7. Marko Modiano, "Standard English(es) and Educational Practices for the World's Lingua Franca," *English Today* (Vol. 15, No. 4, October 1999), 3.
8. Ibid., 8.
9. Geoffrey Sampson, *Schools of Linguistics* (London: Century Hutchinson, 1987), 50.
10. Robert G. Carlson, *The Americanization Syndrome: A Quest for Conformity* (New York: St. Martin's Press, 1987), 2.
11. Robert C. Pooley, *The Teaching of English Usage* (Champaign-Urbana, IL: National Council of Teachers of English, 1974), 5.
12. Michael Bulley, "There Ain't No Grammaticality Here," *English Today* (Vol. 15, No. 3, July 1999), 40–41.
13. Larry Andrews, *Language Exploration and Awareness: A Resource Book for Teachers* (2nd ed., Mahwah, NJ Lawrence Erlbaum Associates, 1998), 135.
14. Ibid., 136.
15. Ibid.
16. Mary Ellen Snodgrass, *The Great American English Handbook* (Jacksonville, IL: Perma-Bound, 87), 38.

Social Conventions and English Use

In this courtroom you will address me as "Your Honor," or you'll be thrown out and held in contempt of court.

—Judge, *Perry Mason*

As you approach this chapter, remember that one of the primary purposes of language is to communicate ideas. Why, then, do we use expressions like "Hello," "Pleased to meet you," and "Good morning, Miss Smith?" These expressions do not communicate factual content. On the other hand, what would happen if you didn't use these expressions when they were expected?

CONVENTIONS AND RULES

Last night "She Who Must Be Obeyed" (a.k.a., Mrs. Andrews) and I went to her favorite restaurant for dinner. After entering the front door, we waited for the hostess to seat us. After we were seated, our waiter brought us menus and glasses of water. "Would you like a drink while you study the menu?" he asked. We each ordered a glass of wine. "Good choices," our waiter observed, "I'll be back in just a few minutes."

The waiter returned with the wine and asked if we needed more time. "No," my wife replied, "we're ready to order now." "Would you like an appetizer?" the waiter asked. After explaining that we didn't care for an appetizer, we each gave the waiter our orders; the waiter left, promising a rapid return with our dinners.

As you've read the opening paragraphs of this chapter, you may have wondered, "What's the big deal? People do this every day. Why is Andrews sharing this mundane and routine information?"

What makes this narrative so commonplace is that it is plainly describing an episode that is very predictable and is repeated thousands of times every day in the United States. You've experienced this sequence of events many times.

I'm using this illustration to make a point: Our waiting to be seated by the hostess is not a *rule* established by the Federal Food and Drug Administration. It's a *convention*, an informal covenant and common understanding at sit-down restaurants.

Similarly, the waiter's act of bringing us menus and glasses of water is not one of compliance with municipal, state, or federal *rules* or mandates. It is merely a social convention. I have eaten in restaurants on four continents and although waiters around the parts of the globe I've experienced always bring a menu, they don't always bring glasses of water.

Our talk with the waiter was so routine that we barely noticed it; it was *conventional*. Our talk was part of the conventions, the linguistic protocols, of the restaurant business in the United States.

Conventions aren't the same as *rules*, or laws. Some rules I observe are the posted speed limits on residential, county, state, and federal streets and highways. These rules have been established through the deliberative, public policy considerations of elected officials. They're like the rules dictating how and when I file my annual income tax reports, or when I renew the licenses on our automobiles, or when I buy my annual fishing permit.

COMMON SOCIAL CONVENTIONS

In addition to the conventions we follow in restaurants, there are other conventions we observe in other aspects of our social interactions.

As I'm writing this chapter, for example, the person who cleans our house on alternate Fridays has just arrived at the customary time. Vanessa knows that I'm normally at home on Fridays, working at my desk.

Without fail, Vanessa announces her arrival with, "Hi, I'm here." Also without fail, I typically reply, "Hello, Vanessa, glad you're here."

We've repeated this exchange numerous times; it's all but scripted. Our Greeting: Greeting exchange seldom changes. Our habitual, albeit brief, conversation is, nevertheless, an important social event.

First, Vanessa enters the house and announces her presence, which I acknowledge. Imagine how our relationship would be different if she came into our home and immediately began her work; also imagine my ignoring her arrival while I'm concentrating on the papers on my desk.

Our Greeting: Greeting exchange is part of the social paste bonding our relationship. It's *conventional* behavior.

One of the first social conventions many people learn is acquired at school: It's standing in line (or standing *on* line as the British might say). Whether it's at day care, preschool, kindergarten, or in the first grade, children are taught early in the culture I know to stand in line (called **queuing** in some cultures), for snacks, drinks at the water fountain, or walks to the cafeteria.

Queuing, like the restaurant conventions described earlier, may seem mundane, but I believe standing in line, like so many other social conventions, is grounded on a basic societal value.

The practice of standing in line began during World War I and II in Great Britain and was subsequently adopted as *conventional* social practice in other English-speaking countries like the United States, and several European countries.[1]

Why do we queue, stand in line? There are a couple of social theories attempting to explain this practice. One hypothesis suggests that in cultures where *time* is valued, people stand in line for whatever service they expect. For example, one study found that in Brazil, where people do not ordinarily stand in line, there are fewer watches and clocks sold, per capita, than in similarly developed countries.[2]

Another theory explaining the convention of queuing is a culture's value given to equality. In some Arab and African countries, for example, women hold social positions inferior and subordinate to men. In those cultures, it is fairly common for men to cut in front of women at bus stops, or other places where queues might form.[3]

In Israel, a more complicated queuing convention is observed. Generally, Israelis oppose regimented behavior of any type, favoring a social value of equality, parity, and equivalence. Therefore, Israelis will not form queues at bus stops. When the bus arrives, however, the riders board the bus in the order of their arrival at the bus stop, following the first-come, first-served principle.[4]

Queuing behaviors, then, vary from one culture to another, and, like most other social conventions, are based on the values of the culture.

In the culture I know, for example, I am expected to eat with a knife, fork, and spoon. My culture doesn't normally use chopsticks or fingers, unless we're eating easily recognized exceptions, like pizza, popcorn, or other finger foods at parties.

If you're not concerned about the social tax we've discussed, you can test what I'm describing here. The next time you're eating in the school cafeteria, try eating your meatloaf and mashed potatoes with your fingers; or, the next time you buy some popcorn at the movie theater, ask for a knife and fork. The test results will be relatively clear, I suspect.

You know, on the other hand, that some cultures use chopsticks, not knives, forks, and spoons. In Ethiopia, it's common practice to use a knife for slicing meat, then use the fingers to eat the meat. In Nigeria, eating an entire meal with one's fingers is conventional behavior, especially if the entrée is yam, which is not the same thing as the North American sweet potato.

When I enter my church, I always remove my winter hat. In the culture I know best, this is an act of respect. Women, on the other hand, aren't constrained by this convention. Although Protestant men conventionally remove their hats in church as a sign of respect, an Orthodox Jew will wear a hat (a yarmulke) covering his head while he is in synagogue, and this, too, is a sign of respect. Here are examples of two different cultures following two different conventions in order to demonstrate the same value.

In the United States, people usually follow relatively stringent conventions governing how close they stand to other people. Unless we're standing beside someone with whom we are on intimate terms, we usually observe the "arm's length" principle. We tend to guard our space, for a variety of reasons. Latinos, Italians, and the French, on the other hand, are more comfortable talking at a much closer space than are U.S. men.

Neither convention can claim to be more or less correct, in the absolute sense. The different conventions merely reflect different sociocultural values [5]

CONVENTIONAL TELEPHONE BEHAVIORS

Social conventions apply to many aspects of our lives, including how we use the telephone. When I answer the telephone at home, for example, I will usually pick up the receiver and say either *Hello* or *The Andrews*. In my culture, either of these answering gambits is equally acceptable by society. In Great Britain, on the other hand, a residential telephone will more likely be answered in a different way. My friend Graham Shaw (OBE), who lives in Barnes, a southwest suburb of London, answers his home telephone with *Hullo; this is seven, eight, nine, four*. Instead of using the U.S. convention of *Hello*, or *The Shaws*, Graham gives the caller the final four digits of his home telephone number.

When I was satisfied that our friendship would permit discussions of social conventions, I described to Graham our different telephone-answering customs. When I asked if he ever used only *Hello,* or *The Shaws,* he replied in a typically British fashion that I've come to enjoy, *Larry, it simply isn't done that way.*

Non-English-speaking countries and cultures follow different telephone-answering conventions.[6] For example, a typical telephone call to a home in Spain will sound like the following (please note that Miguel has placed a call to Carmen):

[Carmen's telephone rings.]

Carmen: *Diga* ("Tell," or "say," a formal command)

Miguel: ¿*Está Javier?* ("Is Javier there?")

Carmen: *Sí.* ¿*Quién es?* ("Yes. Who is this?")

Miguel: *Soy Miguel.* ("I am," or "this is Miguel.")

Carmen: *Sí. Un momento. Ahora se pone.* ("Yes, One minute. He will be here soon.")

Carmen: [calling to Javier] *Javier, ponte. Es Miguel.* ("Javier, come [to the phone]. It's Miguel.")

In Spain, the person answering the telephone begins the conversation in a tone more formal than what is expected in the United States. Note that Carmen begins with *Diga* ("Tell," or "Say"). Carmen might also have answered with *Dígame* ("Tell me") and she would have been conventionally correct. Both *Diga* and *Dígame* are commands for the caller to speak. Either of these two acceptable answers are used with either residential or business telephones in Spain.

In other Spanish-speaking countries, on the other hand, the initial Greeting can vary. In Mexico, for instance, the one receiving the call will conventionally answer with *Bueno* ("Good," or "Well"). Other common telephone greetings in Latin America can be either *Hablame* ("Talk to me") or *Aloh* (Spanglish for "Hello").

Although these conventions may seem curt or brusque to a caller more familiar with U.S. telephone conventions, remember that the telephones in most Spanish-speaking countries are extremely expensive, so costly in fact that many homes have no telephone.

There is a toll assessed for each local call, and the cost is calculated by the minute, like long-distance calls in the United States. Spanish telephone conventions reflect this aspect of the economic culture and, therefore, telephones are used sparingly. The telephone users transact their business quickly, and frugally, reserving their informal talk for cheaper, face-to-face meetings.

BUSINESS TELEPHONE CONVENTIONS

In the United States, different conventions are used when answering a business telephone. The answerer begins the conversation by identifying the business or organization, as in *Good morning, Angst Middle School*, or *Good afternoon, First Methodist Church*, or, as my barber answers his telephone, *Trendsetters; this is Don.*

Some business telephones, I've observed, are answered with an excruciatingly long and overly chummy answer, as in *Thank you for calling Waldo's, now open 24-hours a day at three locations in Pleasantville for your shopping convenience. This is Waldo. How can we help you?*

The contrast between U.S. business and residential telephone conventions is something you've observed, I'm sure. You can test the power of these conventions by misusing them. The next time you answer your home telephone, try something like *Thank you for calling the Ambersons, Art, Alice, Angelique, and Allan. Your call is important to us. How can we help you?*

On the other hand, if you answer the telephone at the business where you work with a Sylvester Stallone-styled *What?*, I'd recommend that you have your résumé updated. You'll be on the job market soon!

You've no doubt noticed that some businesses have replaced the human operator at their central switchboard with a computer-managed answering system. If you call a larger business today, you may be greeted with something like *You've reached the offices of Lotta Bucks Real Estate. If you're calling from a touch-tone phone and know the extension of the party you are calling, please enter that number now. If you want to speak to an agent, please press 1 now. If you have an inquiry about one of our current listings, press 2 now. If you need tax information, press 3 now. If you need title*

*information, press 4 now. If you need survey information, press 5
now. If you have other needs, remain on the line and your call will be
answered soon.*

Computer-managed answering and call-routing systems
are no longer new. Some people appreciate their efficiencies
and others think they are tedious and impersonal. You be your
own judge. Although these automated systems have their own
protocols, I don't know that they really fit into our discussion of
conventions. They are, however, so widespread that I thought
they deserved mention.

DISCOURSE ROUTINES IN CONTEXT

The definition of **Good English** offered in this textbook heavily
relies on *context of use*. What constitutes "Good English" in my
view, must be determined on a case-by-case analysis, which
will include the *individuals* sharing linguistic space with each
other; their social or political *relationship*; the *setting*; the *topic*;
and the *communicative purpose(s)* of the exchange. The language
choices we make are shaped by the total context of use, and the
success of those choices can be determined only by analyzing
all the features of the context.

To believe, however, that a speaker might say to herself,
*Since I'm only going to the supermarket for a loaf of bread and a gallon
of milk, I can leave my "telephone voice" at home* is to misinterpret
how context works. It is seldom that simple or overt for native
English speakers. It is, on the other hand, worthy of special attention with ENL learners. For most of the ENL learners I have
either observed or taught, learning *how* to say English words is
often easier to learn than is learning *when* they are appropriate.

This is especially true for older ENL students who have already acquired a foundation of socially appropriate conventions and accompanying language uses from their native
culture and language.

To illustrate this point, let me share with you an experience I
had with one of my graduate students, a visiting student from
the Middle East. He was one of the PhD students in a doctoral
seminar examining "World Englishes." To celebrate the up-

coming spring vacation at the university, I invited the students and their significant others to my home for an evening of good food and good conversation. The students had been working hard; it was time for a party.

My invitation to the class bothered this student. He remained after class one day in order to explain how sorry he was that he and his wife would not be able to attend the dinner party. "I am greatly embarrassed," he began. "In my country it is the student's duty to invite the professor [He probably spoke a capital "T" and a capital "P," as in The Professor] to dinner in my home first. I have not done this with you and I am ashamed."

I tried to explain, as gently and as reassuringly as I could, that in the United States it is very common for the professor to take the initiative. He was somewhat relieved, but still uncomfortable.

Unwittingly, I had violated a convention known to him. It took him a while to resolve this matter, but, to give this story a happy ending, he and his wife attended the party and, as best I could tell, had a good time.

Whether it's the student or the teacher who initiates a social appointment is a matter of small import to those of you from the culture I know. This episode may seem insignificant to you. Let me tell you, however, it was *not* insignificant to my student! I am sharing this story in an attempt to illustrate how invisible yet powerful social conventions can be.

SOCIAL DISCOURSE CONVENTIONS

In addition to those social routines that determine appropriate etiquette in a culture, there are similar conventions governing appropriate ways to talk in a culture, and I'm not referring to *good grammar*. Even those native English speakers who are unaware of SAE **usages** will be able to observe the **use** of SAE social discourse conventions.

This fact is either frequently ignored or conveniently forgot by traditional English usage handbooks. These handbooks usually offer examples of English-language usage, typically single-sentence icons of "Good English" that are devoid of any context. This is dishonest and unfair, inasmuch as most of the social discourse we participate in is created through connected discourse, in which Statement 1 leads to Statement 2, which leads to Statement 3, and so on. Clearly, most people I know do not wander the globe making one-shot, single-unit observations about the universe.

The single sentence, as Hoey reminded us, is only a small cog in a much larger machine.[7]

To illustrate, here's a brief interchange from yesterday. The exchange is simple, but note especially how even the simplest of statements are *connected*: When I arrived at church yesterday I met Mr. C. O. ("Boots") Shepard.

Exchange 1:

 (1) Boots: Hey, Larry. How're you?
 (2) Larry: Great, Boots. You?
 (3) Boots: Can't complain.
 (4) Larry: Keep it that way.
 (5) Boots: [chuckling] I'm workin' on it.

Simple social exchanges like this are so commonplace that we barely notice them. My point in using this particular illustration is to demonstrate, nevertheless, how we seldom, if ever, make one-sentence statements.

Similarly, other exchanges might be more involved, like the one I participated in last night when my friend Gene Crump called me on the telephone.

Exchange 2:

[Telephone rings.]
 (1) Larry: Hello?
 (2) Gene: Larry, it's Gene.
 (3) Larry: Hi, Gene.
 (4) Gene: Are you busy tomorrow?
 (5) Larry: Yes, I'm at home tomorrow, writing.
 (6) Gene: That's right. I remember now.

(7) Larry: Why? What's up?

(8) Gene: Could you meet with Stephanie and me ?

(9) Larry: Well … sure … as long as it's late afternoon.

(10) Gene: We need to discuss the proposal.

(11) Larry: We definitely need to meet. What time?

(12) Gene: How about 4:00 in your office?

(13) Larry: I'm available.

(14) Gene: Okay; we'll see you then.

(15) Larry: Fine. Take care.

(16) Gene: Right. Bye.

These two exchanges of connected language are mundane and ordinary. They are examples of direct speech requiring little interpretation, although you would appreciate them a bit more, perhaps, if you knew more about my social relationships with Mr. C. O. Shepard and Gene Crump. Nevertheless, these exchanges represent hundreds of similar conversations you and I participate in every week.

For example, in Exchange 1, Mr. Shepard offers in utterance (1) an *Opening Sequence*. In the culture I know, conversations are opened in socially recognized and approved ways. In this case, the Opening Sequence is a *Greeting*. A Greeting like *Hey, Larry. How're you?* is one method we have in our society of implicitly saying, "I recognize you. I want to acknowledge you."[8] Very little substantive content is communicated. A lot of social import is.

Because politeness is a quality valued in many societies, the second speaker is conventionally required to respond to the first speaker's Greeting in a mannerly and courteous fashion. This requirement is met, I believe, in my utterance (2).

The five statements seen in Exchange 1 are ordinary and formulaic, conveying very little information. They should not, however, be undervalued because these five statements, and others like them that are repeated hundreds of times every day, provide much of the paste that helps to hold our society together. If I had ignored Mr. Shepard's Greeting, his feelings would have been hurt, something I do not want to happen.

Exchange 2 illustrates a different kind of Opening Sequence, an *Identification*. In this exchange, Gene employs Identification when he says in (2), *Larry, it's Gene.*

Identification helps, obviously, to identify the speaker, a convention followed by callers whether the call placed is social or business-related. In business-related calls, Identification also helps to gain the answerer's attention, as in a call I received just 2 minutes ago: "Hello, Mr. Andrews. This is Larry Hergert at Williamson's Oldsmobile." His Identification opener gained my attention and helped to establish our conversational agenda: He has an automobile he thinks I might like to purchase.

Using an Opening Sequence–Identification convention in telephone conversations is common in the White U.S. culture, but it is not as often adhered to in the African-American culture, as I know it. When an African-American caller initiates a telephone conversation, he or she is just as likely to begin the conversation immediately after the answerer says "Hello."

For example, last Saturday my university's football team was struggling to keep up with another team, a 23-point underdog. My friend Joan Rich, an avid football fan who is an African American, called me. The telephone rang, I answered with the customary "Hello," and the caller (Joan) began with "What's wrong with our Huskers today? I'm nervous about this game! I wish this game wasn't on TV, then we wouldn't have to watch and worry."

Note that she didn't use an Opening Sequence. Note there's no Identification, "Hello, Larry, it's Joanie." She cuts to the chase and simply begins talking.

Why this difference?

The White culture values good manners. When a White person places a telephone call, it is considered polite to identify oneself. The African-American culture values good manners, too, but also ascribes a very strong value on *community* and *solidarity* among *family*. Consequently, an African-American caller will likely skip the Opening Sequence because identifying oneself is unnecessary. The person receiving the call is *expected to recognize* the caller's voice. The Identification of the caller is *assumed*, it is a *given*.

Another African-American friend who calls me often will begin our telephone conversations using an intimate Opening Sequence. When he calls me and I answer with the conventional "Hello," he opens with "Hey, brother."

David and I grew up in the same town in Missouri many years ago. We delivered papers for the same newspaper, and we played baseball together each summer. Many years later, we are coincidentally living in the same city, attending the same church, singing in the same church choir, and regularly seeing each other at the same social events. His telephone Opening Sequences recognize this shared history and shared present. In the past decade, he has called me hundreds of times and he has never used "Hello, Larry, it's David" as an Opening Sequence. He assumes, correctly, that I will recognize his voice.

ADJACENCY PAIRS

As you've seen in the first three chapters of this book, language is structured in multiple ways. Terry Piper reminded us that language is comprised of "sounds that are strung together to make words that are strung together to make sentences that are strung together to form discourse."[9]

As the current chapter suggests, this "stringing together" is seldom random; it follows conventions that govern the combining of sounds, words, and sentences. [10]

Adjacency Pairs are structural mechanisms society has found useful for organizing social discussions and conversations.[11] Here are several commonly used Adjacency Pairs, with illustrations:

Question–Answer Pair:
  Speaker 1: Have you seen my car keys?
  Speaker 2: Yes, they're on the bureau.

Invitation–Acceptance Pair:
  Speaker 1: Can you meet me for coffee?
  Speaker 2: Yes, I'd like that.

Assessment–Disagreement Pair:

Speaker 1: Fred's Diner has great food.

Speaker 2: You don't eat out often, do you?

Apology–Acceptance Pair:

Speaker 1: I'm sorry I interrupted you.

Speaker 2: No problem. You made a good point.

Summons–Acknowledgment Pair:

Speaker 1: Hey, Jude.

Speaker 2: Yes?

Adjacency Pairs are structured, not randomly organized. They follow a prescribed sequence if conversations are to be successful and, given our earlier definition of Good English, comfortable to the participants.

Notice that the pairs are *contiguous*, and they are spoken by at least two speakers. If a speaker disturbs the conventional sequence in any pair, the result will likely be consternation, confusion, or anger.

Take, for example, the question posed in the previous example: "Have you seen my car keys?" If Speaker 2 answers with "My elbow hurts and it might snow. You know, I still haven't been able to reach Mother on the telephone. I wonder what her weather's like. Yes, on the bureau." Would this exchange cause consternation, confusion, anger, or all of the above?

On the other hand, there is some room for negotiation in the Answer part of this pair. When Speaker 1 asks, "Have you seen my car keys?," it's acceptable for Speaker 2 to Answer with "You're having trouble keeping track of your things. Yes, they're on the bureau."

Also, notice that Adjacency Pairs are *ordered precisely*. Questions always precede Answers (unless you are Alex Trebek!). Invitations precede Acceptances, and we usually don't accept an apology until one is offered.

Similarly, the pairs are always *matched*. It would be an exercise in conversational futility, for example, for the first part of one of these pairs to be followed by the second part of another pair, as in:

Speaker 1: Have you seen my car keys?

Speaker 2: No problem. You made a good point.

UTTERANCE PAIRS

Utterance Pairs are similar to Adjacency Pairs. Utterance Pairs are conversational sequences, too, and the first utterance calls for a prescribed and conventional response. Although you may not have used this terminology, you are familiar the following Utterance Pairs:[12]

Greeting:	Greeting
Question:	Answer
Complaint:	Excuse, Apology, or Denial
Compliment:	Acknowledgment
Farewell:	Farewell

These Utterance Pairs operate in U.S. society much as you would predict. Let's look at the first pair, Greeting:Greeting. When the first speaker offers a Greeting, the second speaker is expected to reply with a corresponding Greeting. If the first speaker offers a Greeting that is either not responded to or is responded to in a socially unapproved manner, there's a communications crash because the Utterance Pair convention has been violated.

If my secretary, the Dutiful Diane, greets me as I enter the office with "Good morning, Larry," my socially approved reply, "Good morning, Diane," is rather formulaic, but important. It's social paste, remember. On the other hand, if her "Good morning, Larry" Greeting is met with "Oh, yeah, who gives a damn?" then I've broken an important social covenant (which I will never do with her.).

There are many ways a speaker can offer a Greeting, depending on *who* is saying *what* to *whom* for what *purpose(s)*. You'll recall this paradigm from chapter 3.

What this paradigm means, when applied to social discourse, is that the initial Greeting may be very formal, semiformal, businesslike, informal, or downright intimate. There's a big difference between "Good morning, Father Downing" and "Good morning, sweetie," but either one can be Good English, depending on the context of use.

No matter which one of these (or other) Greetings is used, however, the first Greeting conventionally requires another Greeting in reply. Similarly, a Question prescribes an Answer, and a Complaint requires an Excuse, Apology, or a Denial. To avoid or to misuse the second half of the Utterance Pair is to invite social, business, or domestic disaster.

One of the more profound features of oral language as it's used in society is the *compulsion* to reply to the first speaker in any of the Utterance Pairs described here, no matter what. Not only does this seem to be true for face-to-face conversations, but it also seems to be true for telephone conversations.

Why else, for example, would we interrupt getting dressed, watching a good video, mowing the lawn, reading a good book, or talking with a family member to answer a ringing telephone?

Labov and Fanshell described this requirement or obligation to reply as a **discourse precondition**. The discourse precondition is stated, simply, as: *when questions are asked, the questioner has a right or a duty to ask a question; the one asked has a responsibility or obligation to answer.*[13]

The best test of the validity of this Question:Answer precondition is to observe this Utterance Pair in operation around you in your daily life. I'm sure you've noticed that whenever someone asks a question, there is an overwhelming need to answer it. When we have no Answer to a Question, we feel uncomfortable, uneasy, or possibly stupid.

It is a brave and confident individual who can say, "I don't know" to a simple yes–no question, especially when the predicted reply is either a mere "yes" or "no."

Chaika's research extends the Labov-Fanshell precondition to cover *all* Utterance Pairs. Consequently, according to Chaika, not only does the Questioner have a presumed right to ask a Question, but the Greeter has a right or duty to Greet, a Complainer has a right or duty to Complain, and so on.[14] Chaika's expansion on this concept produces the following, more inclusive preconditions for Utterance Pairs:

1. The first speaker has a right or duty to speaker.
2. The second speaker has a responsibility or obligation to reply.

The application of these preconditions can be seen anytime you are engaged in an Utterance Pair exchange. What happens if you do not reply to the first speaker? These preconditions are also the foundation for the old joke, "Are you still beating your wife?" A question *requires* an answer.

HOW TO SAY "WE'RE FINISHED"

Whether we're talking about Adjacency or Utterance Pairs, the first speaker begins a conversation with what we described earlier as an **Opening Sequence**. As you read earlier in this chapter, there are socially approved ways to begin, or open, conversations.

Similarly, there are socially approved ways we can tell a conversational partner that our conversation is over, without actually saying so in those words. Using an appropriate **Closing Sequence**—bringing the conversation to its conclusion— is just as important as using an acceptable Opening Sequence.

The cultural value we attach to being polite and courteous prevents a direct statement like "I have no more to say. Good-bye." Although this comment may, in fact, be true, we don't use it because if we did we'd sound impolite, discourteous, curt, rude, or possibly arrogant.

Instead, we use conventions our culture approves of, acceptable code words, to signal a conversational close. Some Closing Sequence code words you've heard, and probably used, include *So, ...*; *Well, ...*; and *Okay, ...* How often have you heard "So, I think that's about it."? Or, "Well, I'll let you go."?

Some Closing Sequences are more elaborate and are couched in other cultural values. For instance, not only does our culture value being polite and courteous, it also values industry, being busy, having things to do. The combination of these values will lead to Closing Sequences like, "Oh my, gosh! Just look at the time. I've got to go because I have more errands to run." Or, "What? It's 9:00 already? I'd better hurry or I'll miss my next appointment."

The second speaker will typically reply to these more elaborate Closing Sequences with something like, "Yeah, I need to go, too." The second speaker doesn't want to appear to be an idler and this is the second speaker's way of saying *I'm busy, too.*

Understanding how conversations are structured in socially approved ways is an important attainment for the ENL learner, as you can appreciate. Although some of the discussion about discourse conventions may strike you as minute, atomistic, or clearly obvious, it is critically important for the ENL learner. These conventions are part of the sociolinguistic paste holding society together.

Be a linguist. Based on what you know and what you have read, summarize some discourse conventions observed in the United States for these speech events:

1. Parent–teacher conference.
2. Sitting beside a member of the clergy in an airplane.
3. An interview with a prestigious school district.

TERMS OF ADDRESS

Native English speakers learn, often indirectly and implicitly, but sometimes as a result of direct intervention by their parents or older caregivers, when it is appropriate to use another person's first name, last name, title, or some other term of address. These conventions, like many of the other conventions examined here, are also based on cultural values.

For example, at the university where I studied for my PhD, all graduate students spoke both *to* and *about* their professors as "Dr. Artley," "Dr. Woods," "Dr. Voth," and so on. When the professors spoke to the graduate students, it was always "Mr. Andrews," "Mr. Guenther," "Mr. Paden," and "Mizz Proctor." (The *Mizz* was used to cover either *Miss* or *Mrs.*)

These were the terms of address conventions adhered to at one university. They were the conventions I learned and followed.

You can imagine, I'm sure, how shocked I was during my first week at my first university appointment when a graduate student came to my office door and said, "Larry, a group of us is going to lunch. Would you like to join us?"

What? You're calling me *Larry*? Have you no respect?

In time I came to understand that conventions governing terms of address in académè vary from campus to campus.

Cultures will also use different terms of address for family relationship titles. As I reminded my in-laws in a speech at their 50th wedding anniversary celebration, "First they call you 'Da-Da;' then they call you 'Daddy;' then they call you 'Dad;' then they call you collect."

In the central-Missouri culture I grew up in, parents were called "Mommy," "Mother," "Mom," "Father," "Daddy," or "Dad." Parents were *never* addressed by their first names. In other parts of the United States, parents might be referred to as "Ma'am," or "Sir," but never by their first names.

You might possibly know of a family whose children call their parents by their first names. Mr. C. O. Shepard, a man you met earlier in this chapter, is widely known in our city as "Boots," a nickname he's had since childhood. All of his nine children and their spouses call him "Boots." This permission does not, however, extend to the grandchildren, all of whom refer to him as "Grandpa."

Richard C. Hudson, an internationally recognized linguist at the University of London's University College, recently surveyed the members of the Language and Culture Discussion Group on the Internet. Based on the results of his survey, Hudson concluded that addressing senior family members by their first names is still not the norm and is likely a minority practice.[15]

CLASSROOM DISCOURSE

When I was a visiting professor at the University of London, I had the opportunity to visit and observe a number of classrooms in the Greater London area, as well as in Wales. In many classrooms, the students would stand when the teacher entered the room. As the teacher walked toward her desk at the front of the room, she would say, "Good morning, fourth form." The students would reply, "Good morning, Miss," and then sit down. This practice was not universal, but it was frequent.

I suspect you'd encounter dogged resistance if you attempted to establish this classroom practice as a new convention in your school in the United States. What's conventional in one culture isn't necessarily conventional in another!

I'm sure you've had the opportunity to overhear children "play school." From these observations, you know that children can assume several "play school" roles, like Teacher, Rowdy Student, and Good Student with relative ease. After having been in classrooms for only a brief period of time, children learn, often implicitly and indirectly, the conventions of classroom talk.

Recent research describing classroom discourse is rather gloomy. I offer the following summaries as descriptions of what has been observed, not what is recommended.

First, Edwards and Mercer concluded one of their reports by noting that "across a wide range of teachers, classrooms, and countries, teachers perform over 76% of the total talk [in classrooms]."[16]

Second, not only do teachers talk a lot in classrooms, Forestal found that when teachers are talking, 60% of the time they're asking questions. Furthermore, the majority of these questions are what Forestal called "display questions," questions for which there is only one expected answer, the answer known by the teacher.[17]

Third, students do not have much time to formulate an answer to a teacher's question. Forestal found that teachers typically allow their students *one second* to answer a question.[18] What kind of question, I ask you, can be answered with only one second wait time? A question that doesn't need to be asked.

The research on classroom discourse hasn't appreciably changed in 40 years or more, dating back to the earlier work of researchers like Ned Flanders, Frank Guszak, and Bruce Biddle. We teachers must love the sound of our own voices! But, if we do, we are sacrificing the needs of an interactive classroom.

This research is especially important when the ENL class-room is considered. Students who are learning English as a new language *must* have opportunities to practice producing language. They'll never have these opportunities if their teachers display *their* English language proficiencies.

THE COOPERATIVE PRINCIPLE

Beyond the walls of our classrooms, whether we're at church, mass, synagogue, the mall, talking over the backyard fence or the bridge table, our social conversations take place with so little effort that we seldom think of the *structure* of these linguistic constructions. we usually focus on their content. Nevertheless, our social conversations are structured in intricate ways, just like the other social conventions examined in this chapter.

Illustrating how conversational partners implicitly work together, illuminating many of the subtleties of oral communication, Paul Grice defined and described what he called "The Cooperative Principle." According to Grice, the principle works in this manner:

> Make your conversational contribution such as is required at the stage at which it occurs, by the accepted purpose or direction of the talk exchange in which you are engaged.[19]

On the face of it, the Cooperative Principle seems clear enough. In order to clarify the principle's nuances, however, Grice offered these additional categories, all a part of the principle.

Category of Quantity. In this category, Grice suggested, the amount of talk in the exchange is important. Ostensibly cooperative conversationalists are expected and assumed (a) to provide as much information as is required, but (b) to provide no more information than is required.[20]

For example, if I ask my secretary, Dutiful Diane, "Were you able to find the type of ink cartridge I need for my printer?" and she replies, "Yes," then I can assume that everything is right with my computer and the world. Should I discover later that Diane bought the *last* of the ink cartridges I prefer, and that the office supply store where my favorite cartridges are sold is going out of business, and I'm going to have to find a new place to buy ink cartridges or buy a new printer and deal with all of the reconfiguration hassles, then I might rightfully wonder why Diane didn't tell me everything. I might feel deceived. Diane would've violated the **Quantity** category because she didn't tell me enough.

On the other hand, the Category of Quantity can be violated in the other extreme, as well. As you have no doubt experienced, some conversational colleagues are truly enamored with the sound of their own voice and will provide you with more, oh, so much more, information than you want. If I ask Diane "Were you able to find the type of ink cartridge I need for my printer?" and she replies with something like "Well, yes I did, and Larry you should visit that new Opulent Office Megamart because they have hundreds of printer cartridges, all you'd ever want to see or buy, and my cousin works there, you know, the cousin who sings with that country western band The Range Rovers? Well, they're playing at Don't Rock the Juke Box, that new country western bar on Broadway this weekend and Mom and I are going. You should take Ruthie. The Range Rovers know all of today's hits and my cousin sounds just like Faith Hill, you know, the singer married to that McGraw guy ...."

Whoa! Please, what about the cartridge?

Those who violate the Category of Quantity might be known as close-mouthed, dull, talkative, or boorish. They will experience a harsh social tax because they aren't cooperative conversationalists.

Diane, by the way, would never conduct herself like the Diane in these illustrations.

Category of Relation. This category is used by Grice to define and describe another important component in cooperative conversations: What is said in the talk exchange will be relevant to the topic.[21]

A simple Question–Answer Utterance Pair, described earlier, can illustrate a successful Category of Relation reply. If I ask my wife, "Have you seen my appointment book?" and she replies "Yes, it's on the top of your bureau," her reply is germane, it's relevant to the question. On the other hand, if she replies with something like "My shoulder is still hurting every time I lift my arm. What's wrong, do you think? Should I go see my physician and have this bursitis looked after?"

Well, I'm sorry about the bursitis, but at the moment I'm looking for my appointment book; I needed to leave for campus 5 minutes ago. Can we discuss the bursitis later this evening? So, I repeat my question, "Have you seen my appointment book?" "You know," my wife might continue, "Mother had bursitis just like this. Maybe I should call her. Are they home today, do you know? I know you talked to Dad last night. Wasn't he going fishing with Uncle Lewis today? What would you like for dinner?"

Nonrelevant contributions violate the Category of Relation, as these purely hypothetical examples illustrate.

Category of Manner. The description of this category characterizes conversational contributions that are clear and orderly. Some helpful synonyms might be "organized" or "cohesive."[22]

Last Saturday night my wife and I went to dinner at a new restaurant with our frequent dining-out friends, Jim and Vickie Sohl. We were seated, unfortunately, by an extremely loud trio we called "The Three Mouthketeers." We weren't eaves dropping, because this group was so loud that even a clam could have overheard their dinner conversation. One of the trio, "The Biggest Mouthketeer," made the following nonstop contributions to their table talk: "Upset? You bet! Not bothered, though. Tough. Real tough. Can take it and handle it. Why? Sod-buster tough. Don't tread on me."

If these comments were organized or cohesive, I'm Babe Ruth.

Category of Quality. We expect our conversational partners will contribute the truth, and we fully expect that a conversation will not be salted with untruths.[23]

Even when a conversational partner has implicitly observed all of the other categories, if we suspect that he or she is "shading the truth," then the whole conversation breaks down. Do you know those whose conversational comments are, to put it most generously, *questionable.*

I know a man whose personal finances are, at best, extremely limited. He's a borderline pauper, I'm sorry to say. For a variety of reasons, however, he is constantly referring to his fashion business, conveniently located in another state, as a "million-dollar enterprise"; the websites he has created, and the millions of dollars he realizes from these developments, and so on. When he speaks about his riches, those around him try to be polite listeners, but they roll their eyes and give each other *there-he-goes-again* looks. Those within the range of his voice don't believe his reports about the businesses he claims to own; consequently, they don't believe anything else he talks about, either.

There are other times, on the other hand, when a violator of the Quality category suffers the same fate, but not because of misrepresentations of fact. For example, there are frustrated, stand-up comedians who are compelled to offer comments they believe to be witty, funny, or especially clever about any conversational topic. People like this become known as the group clown; you've recognized these contributors with comments like, "Can't you ever be serious?" In time, their conversational contributions may be taken for what they are, but in the long run their asides are ignored.

COOPERATIVE PRINCIPLE VIOLATIONS

The Cooperative Principle is routinely violated, as you've probably observed in your daily linguistic life. The more serious violators become known either as windbags, or liars.

Some violations, on the other hand, are not as serious, but are characteristic of the speech we use with those who are on familiar or intimate terms with us. This is another example of where the distinctions between the *form* and the *function* of language become important.

For example, some Questions rendered like Questions really aren't Questions. When my wife asks if I'd like pot roast, potatoes, carrots, and onions for Sunday dinner, and I reply "Is the

Pope a Catholic?", I'm *not* asking a Question. I'm making a statement of affirmation!

Answering a Question with another Question may be a *technical* violation of the Cooperative Principle, but in everyday talk we do it all the time with our regular and intimate conversational partners.

Similarly, what might appear as a violation to an "outsider," really isn't a violation. To illustrate, just last night my wife and I had the following, albeit brief, conversation:

(1) [Telephone rings.]
(2) Ruthie: [calling upstairs] Honey, phone for you.
(3) Larry: I'm just out of the shower.
(4) Ruthie: Okay.

As Widdowson explained, the foregoing conversation is *not* a violation of the Relevance category. [24]

My response "I'm just out of the shower" makes no relevant comment to "Telephone for you," Similarly, there are no cohesive links or ties connecting these comments. The intended communication, however, *given the context,* is successful. Bystanders, who might not understand this exchange, simply don't share "insider" understandings and talk.

Indirect discourse can also be confounded by cultural values. For example, classroom teachers in the United States who have been schooled about the political correctness of democratic, nonauthoritarian talk may "ask" a class, "Will you please get your portfolios now?" This really isn't a Request; it's a Command, disguised as a Request, in order to maintain a feeling of egalitarianism. A student reply of "No, thank you," is not acceptable.

There are several cultural values forcing the teacher to disguise a Command as a Question so that it appears as an invitation. In our culture, we value courtesy and politeness, both in general society and in classrooms.

Teachers and students are expected to be courteous, to be nice, to mind their manners. Teachers are not expected to be dictators; rather, they are expected to be "facilitators" or "organizers of learning opportunities."

Giving a direct command violates these politically correct values. Consequently, all of us teachers disguise our Commands so that we can ostensibly avoid being seen an educator who does not believe in or practice democracy in the classroom. Teachers typically use a more acceptable language *form*, but intend a different language *function*.

Discourse can be disguised to fit social and cultural expectations outside the walls of the classroom, as you've observed

When my wife asks me, "Can you drop these things off at the dry cleaners on your way to campus this morning?" only a total fool would consider replying "I'd rather not, but thanks for asking." Her statement is a Request/Command disguised as a Question.

Why do we disguise Requests/Commands like the dry cleaners statement? In order to avoid appearing to be too bossy, pushy, and the like.

Sometimes we bend over backward to be polite with our Requests/Commands. This disguise can be intensified with the addition of "please," as in "Can you drop these things off at the dry cleaners on your way to campus this morning, *please*?" This disguise is intensified and sweetened even more when it appears as "Can you drop these things off at the dry cleaners on your way to campus this morning, *please, honey*?"

Within the past several days I've heard the following Request/Commands at my house, all of them appropriately disguised as more polite inquiries? "Do you think you should be wearing that old sweater to Susan's dinner party tonight?" "Do you think you'll have time to call the carpet cleaner today?' "Do you think it would be a good idea if we invited the Turners to come home with us for dinner after church next Sunday?"

My range of replies to these Questions is limited!

Requests can also be disguised when we don't want to appear to be forgetful or stupid, and we want to save face. "Where's the library," for example, is not only too direct, but reveals lack of knowledge, and is likely to be disguised as a Question: "Do you know the location of the library?'

Again, a simple "yes" or "no" is usually not an acceptable reply to these Requests disguised as Questions. We know this, implicitly, so we play along with the disguise and reply, "I'm so sorry, but you see, I'm a visitor here myself." Why are we "so sorry?" Because we're mannerly, perhaps compassionate.

Modesty is another cultural value. I'm sure you've noticed that when some people receive a Compliment, they have trouble with the Acknowledgment part of the Utterance Pair. This may be due to their implicit understanding of the modesty value, or it may be a result of their caregivers' admonitions, "It's rude to boast."

Consequently, a Compliment like "What a pretty blouse" or "I just love your shoes" will sometimes elicit an Acknowledgment like "What, this old thing?" or "These shoes are out of fashion, I'm afraid."

It is instructive, I believe, to temper these remarks about social discourse conventions with a brief review because we violate so many of the conventions, with good cause.

We have defined *Good English* as the ability to make appropriate linguistic choices so that the fewest number of participants will be distracted by those choices. Therefore, as we assess the "goodness" of an utterance, we must analyze each interaction on a case by case basis, asking ourselves *who* is saying *what* to *whom* under what *circumstances* for what *purpose*?

Let's take the Compliment–Acknowledgment pair as an example. When I go fishing at Lake Perry with my father-in-law, he will frequently invite a business associate to join us. If I reel in a 14-inch crappie, the "outsider," the invited business associate, might say to me, "Larry, you did a good job bringing in that slab of a crappie." A conventional Acknowledgment to this Compliment might be something like, "Thanks. I was lucky."

If, on the other hand, the fishing party is only my father-in-law and me and I pull in a 14-inch crappie and he says "Larry, you did a good job bringing in that slab of a crappie," then I just might say "Of course. I'm a heck of a fisherman."

It's the *who* is saying *what* to *whom* parts of the paradigm that account for the different Acknowledgments. I usually don't know the invited business associate. Because of our social distance, I'm more likely to use a polite, conventional Acknowledgement to a Compliment.

On the other hand, my more boastful Acknowledgment to my father-in-law's Compliment is based on years of love, respect, and fraternal pleasure in each other's company, not to forget friendly competition when we go fishing. The context determines the "goodness" of the reply.

My experiences with ENL learners lead me to conclude that these language learners can successfully complete any number a workbook pages requiring them to identify grammatical nuances of English. If, however, they cannot understand the indirect, implicit and the "between the lines" communicative intentions used in American English, then their choices in both language and society will be limited.

> *Be a linguist.* The next time you find yourself talking to a telephone solicitor, interrupt the Opening Sequence by asking "What are you selling?" or "What do you want me to buy?" What happens? Why?

FOR DISCUSSION

Part 1. Place a ✓ beside each statement made in the text. Be prepared to cite page numbers in support of your decisions.

___ 1. Social conventions are more culture-specific than are social rules.
___ 2. Social values help to shape social conventions.
___ 3. Those who do not conform to conventions may be admired.
___ 4. Cooperative Principle violators can't be trusted.
___ 5. Conventions are learned from committed caregivers.

Part 2. Place a ✓ beside each statement you believe the text would support. Be prepared to cite page numbers in support of your decisions.

___ 6. Context can affect what we wear and what we say.
___ 7. The relationship between the Cooperative Principle and Discourse Preconditions is substantial.

___ 8. Cohesion in oral discourse is often assumed.

___ 9. An unanswered question is never acceptable.

___ 10. Discourse rules are universal across age groups in a culture.

Part 3. Based on what you know and what you have read in this chapter, place a ✓ beside each statement you can support.

___ 11. Sometimes it is good to keep up with the Joneses.

___ 12. What's new isn't always improved.

___ 13. You're known by the company you keep, or don't.

___ 14. There is no "i" in teamwork.

___ 15. Sell the sizzle, not the steak.

NOTES

1. Malcolm Caldwell, "Queue & A: The Long and Short of Standing in Line" *The Washington Post National Weekly* (December 21–27, 1992), 38.
2. Ibid.
3. Ibid.
4. Ibid.
5. Edward Anthony, "The Rhetoric of Behavior," *TESOL Matters* (Vol. 6, No. 5, October/November, 1996), 23.
6. The discussion of Spanish telephone conventions is based on Sally Andrews, "Spanish Telephone Conventions," in Larry Andrews, *Language Exploration and Awarenes: A Resource Book for Teachers* (2nd ed., Mahwah, NJ: Lawrence Erlbaum Associates, 1998), 164.
7. Michael Hoey, *On the Surface of Discourse* (London: George Allen & Unwin, 1983), 1.
8. Edward Finegan and Niko Besnier, *Language: Its Structure and Use* (New York: Harcourt Brace, 1989), 344.
9. Terry Piper, *Language and Learning: the Home and School Years* (Upper Saddle River, NJ: Prentice-Hall, 1998), 11.
10. Ibid.
11. Finegan and Besnier, 341–344.
12. Elaine Chaika, "Discourse Routines," in Virginia P. Clark et al. (eds.), *Language: Introductory Readings* (New York: St. Martin's Press, 1985), 429–455.

13. William Labov and David Fanshell, *Therapeutic Discourse: Psychotherapy as Conversation* (New York: Academic Press, 1977), 81–82.
14. Chaika, 436.
15. Richard C. Hudson, "Naming Practices," Language & Culture LIST-SERVE, <u>language-culture@uchicago.edu</u>, July 11, 1995.
16. David Edwards and Norman Mercer, *Common Knowledge: the Development of Understanding in the Classroom* (London: Heinemann, 1987), 20.
17. Peter Forestal, "Talking: Toward Classroom Action," in Marvin Brubaker, Ronald Payne, and Kenneth Ricket (eds.), *Perspectives on Small Group Learning: Theory and Practice* (Ontario: Rubicon, 1990), 159.
18. Ibid.
19. Paul Grice, *Studies in the Way of Words* (Cambridge, MA: Harvard University Press, 1989), 26.
20. Ibid.
21. Ibid., 27.
22. Ibid.
23. Ibid.
24. Henry Widdowson, *Explorations in Applied Linguistics* (Oxford, England: Oxford University Press, 1989), 138.

CHAPTER 5

American English Variations

You like potato and I like potahto,
You like tomato and I like tamahto
Potato, potahto, tomato, tomahto.
Let's call the whole thing off.
—Ira Gershwin, *Let's Call the Whole Thing Off*

As you approach this chapter, it's time to take inventory of some of your attitudes about English and the people who use it. How do you feel about those who pronounce a word differently from your normal pronunciation? Where and how did you learn these feelings?

In my garage you'll find several shelves, two cabinets, and two vertical fishing rod holders. All of these storage areas are places where I keep a variety of tools, either for home-repair tasks, or for fishing, for automobile cleaning, for carpet spot removal, for mending cracks in the driveway, and the like. Depending on the task I'm facing, I'll try to select the most appropriate tool that will help me to accomplish whatever the job might be.

In my head, on the other hand, I have a word bank. I make withdrawals from this bank when I'm writing a book, or when I'm transcribing a quote from another book, or if I'm writing a note to my wife, or if I'm jotting down a shopping list, or if I'm creating an e-mail message to my brother in Texas. Obviously, I use different words for different language jobs.

In both examples, I'm using instruments, devices, for completing a task.

My friend Larry Routh might use the implements in my tool box differently. My literacy studies compatriot David Wilson might use his word bank differently, too. Other people will exhibit even more differences in their manipulations of the tools, whether the tools are from Sears or the American English lexicon. Quite often, they'll leave their personal mark on the completed task, distinguishing their abilities from the talents of others.

Last weekend, my wife and I went shopping for a new bedroom suite for one of the guest bedrooms. When my wife found one she really liked, she asked the salesclerk, "Who made this?" When the salesclerk gave my wife the manufacturer's name, she turned to me and knowingly offered, "They make quality products."

This manufacturer is, apparently, well-known in the furniture field. "Look at this feature," my wife said to me, as she pulled out a drawer from the dresser. "They always do that."

This furniture manufacturer has a standard attribute, I've learned, in the way it assembles drawers in dressers, bureaus, and chests. It's a trademark feature distinguishing this manufacturer from others.

If you are a music aficionado, you know that composers and performing artists have distinguishing features, too. A jazz fan, for example, will immediately know the difference between a song sung by Ella Fitzgerald or Billie Holiday. Gerry Mulligan's baritone saxophone has a unique sound. Miles Davis and Wynton Marsalis play the same instrument, but the sounds they bring out of their trumpets are different.

Writers and speakers have personalized ways of using language. You're not likely to confuse a poem written by e.e. cummings with one written by Robert Frost.

I gave a copy of one of my earlier books to our friends Jim and Mimi Wickless. One night Mimi stopped reading in mid-page and called to her husband, "Jim, let me read this to you; it sounds just like Larry."

I'm not trying to place myself in the same category with cummings or Frost, please understand! The point is: Whether you're a furniture maker, a musician, a portrait artist, a photographer, a writer, or a speaker, you'll use the tools of the enterprise in uniquely personal and individual ways.

We use the term **idiolect** to describe the language system of an individual as expressed in the way he or she characteristically speaks and writes. Think now of national political figures and the news reporters you watch on television. The senators from your state, the representatives from your congressional district, and the news reporters have ways they characteristically use the language.

It's not just national figures, however, who have idiolects. Each person in the world who uses language will use it in a uniquely personal manner. I know you've observed this when someone recounts an event involving your family, and you reply, "Yes, I can just hear Uncle Frank [or Dad, Aunt Carolyn, Grandma, etc.] saying that."

When we're describing the language of loved ones in our family, we cherish the unique ways they say things. On the other hand, if some people hear a speaker from another part of the country, or another ethnic identity, pronounce a word in a distinctive way, there's a tendency among some of denigrate their language performance. "Did you hear that," they'll sometimes say, "it sounds just like *those* people!"

SOME BELIEFS
ABOUT STANDARD ENGLISH

Tom McArthur described a relatively common position among many linguists when he said that Standard English is a "widely used term that resists easy definition." He goes on by commenting that "Some consider its meaning to be self-evident," while others see Standard English "as a thoroughly inconvenient fiction, built on social elitism and educational privilege.[1]

"Standard English" can be defined as the variety of language use that enjoys the greatest degree of status or prestige in a nation or a community, as it is used by those persons in positions of authority and power. This definition includes public officials, magazine and newspaper writers and editors, school teachers, university professors, priests, pastors, rabbis, and the like. These are individuals who are models in their respective communities.

As you examine this array of language users, and as you reflect on your discussion of **idiolect**, however, you will likely conclude that any definition of "Standard English" will leak.

For example, which of these sentences would you call "Standard English?" *That is not true. That's not true. That isn't true.* Would your selection be helped if you knew whether these sentences were spoken or written? I suspect it would because most people have a greater tolerance for variations in spoken language than they do in written language.

There are those, on the other hand, who are so taken with the idea of "Standard English" that they accept no variations whatsoever. They believe that there is a list, a catalogue, of Good English usages, and that the list never changes. It's the teacher's job to teach, and it's the learner's job to learn this list. Harris called this erroneous belief "the fixed-code fallacy."[2]

Clearly, the definition offered in this book for Good English recognizes that what is appropriate language use in one context isn't necessarily appropriate in another, but that in their respective contexts, seemingly conflicting usages can be Good English. This definition stands in sharp contrast to the "fixed-code fallacy."

In chapter 1, we examined a number of properties of human language as it is distinguishable from the signaling systems of animals. Another property not presented in chapter 1 is germane at this point: **variation**. As you know, American English varies from one region of the country to another. People in Savannah, Georgia, don't pronounce every word just like the people in Savannah, Missouri. What's a *creek* in one locale might be a *crick* in another.

Language also varies from generation to generation. My grandmother, now deceased, never encountered the word *microwave*. To her, a *mouse* was a nasty critter you didn't want around or it was another term for a black eye. A *mouse* as a computer adjunct was totally unknown to her generation, but common to your age.

Language varies according to social class or culture, too. The mid-day meal is called *lunch* by some, *dinner* by others. The evening meal can be either *supper* or *dinner*.

This list of examples could continue, but we'll end it here, believing the point has been sufficiently illustrated. Language used by persons of authority and power, those who set the standard in "Standard English," simply varies too much for us to consider a fixed code of Proper English.

Gere and Smith summarized several public notions about "Standard English," a summary important for us to consider because it captures, I believe, how the general public might use the term:

1. "Standard English" is a clearly definable set of correct pronunciations, grammatical structures, and word choices. It is "standard" because it represents the widest range and because it has been refined to be the most versatile and acceptable form of English.
2. "Standard English" is the kind of language that people should use for all occasions. "Standard" means most serviceable and negotiable and, therefore, most correct.
3. "Standard English" is necessary for success in school and, therefore, in employment. One of the principle reasons for having schools is to equip young people with the skills necessary to improve their chances for social and financial

rewards. Conformity to certain ways of using language obviously underlies many of those skills.

4. "Standard English" is the best version of English for the expression of logical and abstract thought. Because all of the great British and American writers use this form of English and because most of the business in our society is conducted with this form, it must be the form best suited to the expression of precise and sophisticated thought.

5. Some people, like African Americans and hillbillies, speak a version of English that is degenerate. Signs of this degeneracy can be found in their sloppy pronunciation, imprecise vocabulary, and their violation of so many grammatical rules. All of these signs point to a form of language that is inadequate for accurate communication.[3]

As you reflect on these summarized public sentiments about "Standard English," you may find it difficult either to accept or to reject any one of the five summaries in toto. Parts of each statement may look attractive and agreeable to you; other parts of each statement might be more disagreeable. As a language teacher, you need to decide how you feel about these summaries and how they inform your teaching.

AFRICAN-AMERICAN ENGLISH VERNACULAR

Among the general public you'll find those fixed-code adherents who are confident that the roots of "Standard English" are found in the "purer" form of English the colonists brought with them on the Mayflower. Several centuries later, British English is typically admired by speakers and writers of American English; excluding the Cockney variations, a British English accent enjoys considerable prestige in the United States.

Furthermore, even if these people accept the fact that there are regional variations in the ways American English speakers pronounce certain words, down deep they believe that one dialect (usually their own) is preferred, or "standard."

African-American English Vernacular, sometimes referred to as either Black English or Black English Vernacular, is often stigmatized as being "substandard," not Standard American English. Whether African-American English Vernacular is seen as a separate language or a U.S. dialect, it is substandard in the eyes of some.

African Americans have a unique and singular cultural linguistic history in the United States. Their West African ancestors were first brought to this country about a decade after the arrival of the first colonists. The Anglo-European colonists came *voluntarily*, looking for adventure, religious or political freedom, and other opportunities. The West Africans, on the other hand, came *involuntarily*, and could anticipate only a life of slavery.[4]

The slave owners determined not only when the West Africans would come to North America, but also where and under what conditions they would live. Blacks were unable, therefore, to assimilate into the prevalent culture like the Anglo-European colonists could, or to maintain their own traditions and cultures under circumstances of their own choice. No other group of immigrants faced these limitations. Because of these constraints, African-American Vernacular developed differently than did any other language variety in this country.[5]

Nevertheless, there are a number of words currently in the American English vocabulary that are rooted in West African languages, words like *impala, limber, jazz, jumbo,* and *tango*.[6]

As discussed in chapter 2, the American English vocabulary grows and reinvents itself through a number of word-formation processes. You'll recall that some words are **borrowed** from other languages. Some examples of borrowings from West African languages are *goober* (peanut), *chigger, sweet talk,* and *banjo*.[7]

We can conclude, I believe, that while the slaves were learning English words from their overseers, the overseers were learning West African words from the slaves.

After the American Civil War, African-American Vernacular continued to develop. African-American Vernacular, in my judgment, is not a **dialect** of SAE. SAE developed from Anglo-European languages; African-American Vernacular developed from West African languages. Like all other languages,

African-American Vernacular is systematic. Among some of the features that distinguish African-American Vernacular today are the following:

1. The use of *been* to express a past activity with continuing relevance (*I been knowing Mrs. Glass since I was 7 years old.*).
2. No final *-s* in the third person singular tense (*He talk funny.*).
3. Omission of the verb *to be* in the present tense when it is used as a linking verb (*They real good.*).
4. The use of double negative involving the auxiliary verb at the beginning of a sentence (*Ain't never had no black-eyed peas on no piece of lettuce.*).
5. The use of the verb *be* to indicate habitual activity (*She be late to church every week.*).[8]

These examples of African-American Vernacular, all of which I have recently heard, do not represent a language in decline. They represent, given our earlier discussion of the development of African-American Vernacular, an adaptation of English that followed a different route to becoming systematic and regular.

It is important for you to understand, especially if you are not African American, that not all African Americans speak African-American Vernacular. Some speak it all of the time, some speak it some of the time, and some speak it not at all.

Someone born in Boston is not predestined to speak Boston English, whether it's Brahmin, "Hahvid," or "Southie." Similarly, someone born Black is not predestined to speak African-American Vernacular.

Whether a Black person speaks African-American Vernacular is shaped largely by choice, depending on the context, one's social status, and the like.[9] Furthermore, it's very common for many African Americans to switch back and forth between African-American Vernacular and SAE when the context either allows or demands it.

Let me describe four African Americans I know well. One is employed in a professional position in an international pharmaceutical firm. Among her Black female friends are a public school teacher with a Master's Degree, a university professor with a PhD, and a middle-management administrator with a national insurance firm who earned a Bachelor's Degree.

When this group is gathered for a Saturday afternoon session of snacks and card-playing, they shift easily into African-American Vernacular "sista talk" because of the informal and bonding context. They aren't being subversive, shifting from their "professional languages"; they're simply being "sisters," a community.

This linguistic event is not unique to African Americans. All of us shift our language to suit the social circumstance. The languages I use when I'm fishing with neighbor Norman, when I'm teaching a class, when I'm speaking from the pulpit at my church, or when I'm cheering for my university's football team, are different. The differences are *normal*; not making a difference would be *abnormal*.

It is important for your students to understand that they will hear variant pronunciations of certain words, and that some native English speakers will demonstrate slight grammatical differences in their speech. These variations are normal and do not constitute errors.

On the other hand, recall the definition of **Good English** from chapter 3. Good English is marked by the ability to make language choices so that the fewest number of participants will be distracted by those choices. This definition accommodates the overpowering importance of using English which is appropriate to the context, and no question like "Is this correct English?" can, in my view, avoid the consideration of *who* is saying *what* to **whom** under what *circumstance*.

There are, nevertheless, certain uses of English which are socially marked. You are not serving your in a professional manner if you ignore these. As we said in chapter 3, attend to those variations bearing the greatest social stigma.

Be a linguist. Use your dictionary and determine which is "the preferred pronunciation" for the following words: *aunt, orange, garage, root, route,* and *wash.*

PHONOLOGICAL, GRAMMATICAL, AND LEXICAL VARIATIONS

Deciding whether two competing and contrasting variations are either dialects of the same language or two different languages has been a controversial topic, as are almost all language issues. Linguists typically use **mutual intelligibility** as the primary criterion in answering this question.

If two speech varieties are not mutually intelligible, then they're usually considered separate languages. If they are mutually intelligible, then they are considered dialects of the same language.

Understand that there are levels of mutual intelligibility, and, furthermore, it is a sociolinguistic fact of life that some people will claim that they do not understand the speech of others. Judgments like these are often social or psychological comments. Some people want to understand the speech of those they either like or approve of, while they don't want to understand the speech of those they don't like.

In mutually intelligible languages dialect variations usually involve these three features:

1. lexical variations (vocabulary),
2. phonological variations (accent), and
3. grammatical variations.

These are the three aspects of language typically used to describe the more observable variations in dialects. Any of these three features can vary not only from one geographic region to another, but also by social class, gender, age, and occupation. Whether we're talking about lexical, phonological, or grammatical variations, and we ask ourselves "Why do those people use that word?", or "Why do they pronounce that word they way they do?", one of these main reasons is, quite simply, that people who talk *with* one another talk *like* one another.[10]

Lexical Variations. In different parts of the United States, for example, the kitchen utensil used for frying bacon might be called either a *fry pan*, a *frying pan*, a *skillet*, or even a *spider*. Similarly, when visitors enter your home, do they come in to the *living room*, the *front room*, or the *main room*? When people you know go fishing, what do they use for bait, a *fishing worm*, a *night crawler*, a *fish worm*, or an *angle worm*? I've heard people in different parts of the United States ask for directions to the *powder room*, the *bath room*, the *wash room*, the *ladies'* (or *men's*) *room*, the *toilet*, the *lavatory*, the *rest room*, and the *basement*.

There are numerous examples of more lexical variations you can add to this list, I'm sure.

Phonological Variations. These variations are equally as obvious as are lexical variations. You've probably noticed that some people pronounce the word *root* with the same vowel sound heard in the word *put*. On the other hand, some pronounce *root* using the vowel sound heard in *boot*.

I make no distinctions in the pronunciations of *ant* and *aunt*. My wife, on the other hand, does. She pronounces *aunt* using the same vowel sound heard in the word *haunt*. Her pronunciation of *ant* uses the same vowel sound heard in *pant*.

Some people say *greasy*, whereas others render it *greazy*. Some people *wash* the dishes, whereas others *warsh* them, and there are those who *park* the car, but others *pahk* the car.

Any of these pronunciations is as linguistically "good" as another. At the level of meaning, the word pairs are equals and are mutually intelligible. If a preference is indicated for one pronunciation over another, then that's a *social* statement, not a *linguistic* statement.

Grammatical Variations. My niece and nephew, who live in the Southern dialect area of the United States, asked me on the telephone just last night, "Are *y'all* going to be at Grandma's while we're there?" Their use of the second person pronoun *y'all* is at variance with the way I might render the same sentence, "Are *you* going to be at Grandma's?"

Similarly, when I was a recent arrival at the university where I teach today a colleague asked me, "Some of us are going to lunch soon; do you want to go *with*?" I stood there on one leg, waiting for him to complete his sentence! His sentence and its syntax is common, however, among those native to this geographic area.

In British English (BrE) grammar, it's common for the definite article to be omitted where it's required in American English (AmE). A BrE speaker might say, for instance, "I must visit my brother *in hospital* this afternoon." And, another BrE speaker might say, "I thought your son was *at university* this year." These are grammatical expressions in BrE but are not grammatical in AmE.[11]

BrE speakers might say that they will see you "*at* the weekend," whereas an AmE speaker would say "*on* the weekend." Similarly, a BrE speaker might direct you to a store (or, more likely, a *shop*) which is located "*in* Cherrywood Lane. The AmE speaker will say "*on* Cherrywood Lane."[12]

DIALECT INTOLERANCE

There are hundreds of examples of lexical, phonological, and grammatical variations that have not been illustrated in the few examples provided here, all illustrating how modifications in AmE naturally and normally exist.

Dialectologists have been studying variations in AmE for many years and the systematic modifications are so apparent that they can be charted. Examples of how linguistic variations become regional clusters and can be represented on language maps are numerous.[13]

I can't stress this enough: These variations are justifiable and legitimate options for the pronunciations of words, the selections of words, and the grammatical arrangements of words. They illustrate a point made before: People who speak *with* one another speak *like* one another.[14] People naturally accommodate their language habits to those of people with whom they interact.[15]

Nevertheless, despite all the evidence supporting the normalcy of linguistic variation, some people remain intolerant of others who speak a different dialect. There is no logical or linguistic rationale for this sentiment, inasmuch as *any* dialect, including *yours*, can be interpreted as "different" by somebody.

To illustrate this point, remove yourself to another part of the United States and you'll discover that *you* are the linguistically different one!

What are the implications of all this? To put it briefly, would any person make someone else feel *guilty* about the different color of his or her skin? Treat dialect differences with the same degree of sensitivity and humanity.

Few educators will disagree, I suspect, with what I've just written. As Mackey noted, however, "Only before God and linguists are all languages equal."[16]

It is fairly common, therefore, for schools to use the so-called Standard English—the English uses found in textbooks and used in the media—as the school standard. The general assumption is that this is the English needed in order to be successful either in school or in the job market.[17] Standard English is often viewed as more logical, more precise, and sometimes even more elegant than other varieties of English.

The nonstandard varieties are often seen as corrupted or debased forms of English and bear a heavy stigma. Some varieties falling into this category are the social dialects of the working class, some regional dialects (Appalachian, for example), and ethnic or minority dialects, like African-American Vernacular English.[18]

It has been conventional wisdom that allowing the use of these dialects in the classroom will interfere with the learners' ability to acquire Standard English forms. To the surprise, or chagrin, of many, research does not support this view. To the contrary, available research findings indicate incorporating students' vernaculars in the classroom is often a helpful bridge to the learning of the standard forms.[19]

REGIONAL AND SOCIAL REACTIONS TO DIALECTS

When I was a visiting professor at the University of London Institute of Education, my family lived south of the Thames in the "suburb" of Putney. My younger daughter attended school in neighboring Richmond. A gregarious type, Sally would bring home with her many newfound friends for apres-school teenage snacks and adolescent snickering. Numerous times I overheard her British schoolmates ask "Sally, say something in Yank [*Yankee*, AmE]. It's so clever."

Sally always obliged, innate teacher and predestined linguist that she was. She would render AmE words with her broadened /a/ sound or she would pronounce a phonetic /r/ sound in words, often dropped in BrE. Her British schoolmates would squeal in linguistic and cross-cultural delight.

This illustrates, as do the other examples provided in this chapter, I hope, that one variation of English is as useful and as communicative as another. Logic doesn't always rule, however, in language matters. Some varieties are favored and some are stigmatized.

For example, how do you react to the difference between *wash* and *warsh*? Whenever I use *warsh* as an example of language variety in one of my classes, this variant pronunciation will be greeted by some with knowing chuckles and we-know-better-don't-we smiles. *Warsh*, nevertheless, is recognized in most dictionaries as a recognized pronunciation.

Furthermore, to return to a word considered earlier, do you use the word *data* as a singular or a plural noun? I learned, as you've read, to treat it as a plural. Nevertheless, here are two connected sentences I recently encountered in a language text written by a well-known scholar published by one of the world's leading academic presses: "Where, for example, does our data come from? How good is *it*?"[20] (my emphasis).

Granted, *warsh* and *data* are only two examples out of some 100 bazillion words we can choose from, but I use them here to symbolize all of the other and additional variations people might use.

Language variation across social class lines, moreover, is not a recent event. Labov examined this matter several years ago. Having observed that some New Yorkers pronounce the /r/ at the ends of words like *bar, mar, par,* and *tar,* and also observing that some New Yorkers dropped the /r/ at the ends of these same words, Labov investigated his observations in a more precise and controlled manner.

Collecting data in three department stores—one an expensive, upscale store; the second a medium-priced, middle-class store; and the third a discount store most often frequented by working class customers—Labov found that the presence or absence of the postvocalic /r/ was clearly related to the social class of the shoppers at the three stores. Furthermore, the employees at the expensive, upscale store consistently pronounced the postvocalic /r/, but the employees at the discount store did not.[21]

In the United States, dropping the final /r/ had been a practice associated with lower class speakers, whereas pronouncing the final /r/ had been associated with speakers from higher social classes. Labov's data confirmed these observations.

In Great Britain, on the other hand, just the *opposite* seems to be the case with regard to social class and the use of the pronounced final /r/. Speakers of BrE who are affiliated with higher social classes do not pronounce the final /r/, whereas some speakers of BrE from lower social classes do.

The differences between data obtained in New York City and Reading, Great Britain, are revealing, according to Trudgill's research (see Table 5.1).

TABLE 5.1   Pronunciation of Final /r/

Social Class	New York City	Reading, UK
Upper middle class	32%	0%
Lower working class	10%	49%

So, what do these (pluralized!) data help us to understand? Simply, this: in one major city in the United States, *pronouncing* the final /r/ is a characteristic of the upper social classes, but in another major city, this one in Great Britain, *dropping* the final /r/ is a characteristic of the upper social class. What's "in" with one social class is "out" with a similar social class. The socially approved uses of English will vary from one culture to another.

All styles vary from culture to culture. Language is just one style. Clothing styles popular in one culture will be unpopular in another. The same is true with foods. Today, sun-dried tomatoes and cilantro are "in" foods in some cultures, whereas other cultures prefer other food items. Who sets the various styles? The recognized prestige or power figures in the community.

In most societies, some people are treated and greeted with greater deference than others. Those who are either economically, culturally, or politically powerful enjoy greater prestige than those who are less privileged. Consequently, the cars the "in" people drive, the homes they own, the clothes they wear, and the language they use all become "the standard."

Although I understand and appreciate the fact that you may object to this generalization, and that you may believe it's neither just nor fair, I maintain that it is *so*. Given the relationship between behavior and power, certain language uses are often judged as "Good" or "Bad," depending on who uses them[23]

For example, *ain't* was considered at one time as an acceptable contraction for *am not* or *are not*. When *ain't* is used today, however, as a normal part of one's language repertoire, it has become stigmatized and has become a symbol or a marker of substandard speech. (I'm excluding here the use of *ain't* either for emphasis or for humor.)

As Conklin and Laurie described the spontaneous and regular use of *ain't*, "An *ain't* user is judged by society not only to be speaking non-standard English, but to be ignorant, insensitive, dumb, even dirty—stereotypes of lower class people.[24]

Conversely, when speakers use conventional pronunciations, speak without hesitation, and use few, if any pause markers (*like*, you know, *um*, and *ah*, *er*), then they are more likely to be judged by society as more able and more competent speakers, and more socially prominent.[25]

SOCIAL BONDS AND NETWORKS

The dialect patterns people use are the products of numerous environmental factors. For example, we are born into a specific **language network**, a matrix of political, social, economic, religious, and moral beliefs voiced through the phonological, lexical, and grammatical features used by our caregivers: a mother, a father, older siblings, aunts, uncles, neighbors, and the like. The initial language network provides our first models of language use.

It is through these interactions that we learn the social norms for word choices, pronunciation patterns, and grammatical structures. These social norms are learned implicitly and indirectly, seldom from direct instruction. we accommodate our language so that it agrees with those persons we most often interact with.

Be a linguist. Given what you know about how people use language, what is happening to the auxiliary verb *have* in these sentences:

1. She would of told us.
2. He would of driven his car if we had asked him.

LANGUAGE AND CULTURE

The word *dialect* can be modified a number of ways. We can describe a *regional* dialect, a *social* dialect, and we can describe a *cultural* dialect. You have already seen examples of the first two.

An example of **cultural dialect** was recently provided by an acquaintance of mine who was recounting a conversation he had with his son. "I told him," the acquaintance said, "that he owed his mother an apology—a *big league* apology" (my emphasis).

Most of us in the United States can attach some significance to the use if *big league,* as opposed to *minor league,* in this quote because most people in the culture you and I know have at least some rudimentary knowledge of baseball and its terminology. On the other hand, you don't need to strain your brain to think of other cultures where the use of *big league* would be bewildering.

Similarly, my most recent trip to the supermarket reminded me of other cultural language markers. At the check-out counter, the clerk asked me, "Paper or plastic?" As she rang up my total bill, she asked, "Cash or charge?" After I paid my bill for the groceries, she asked, "Drive up?"

Her questions were very formulaic. Did I want her to place my purchases in a paper bag or in a plastic carrier? Did I want to pay cash for my purchases, or did I want to use a credit card? Finally, she was asking whether I planned to carry the groceries to my car, or was I going to drive up to the area where there are supermarket employees who will put the groceries in the trunk of my car? Again, I ask you, can you think of other parts of the world—other cultures—where these questions would make no sense at all?

Furthermore, sports metaphors are good examples of cultural dialect: Can you think of cultures where "hitting below the belt," "It's time to punt," or "Three strikes and you're out" would create no meaning?[26]

HISTORICAL VARIATIONS

Language varies from one regional network to another, from one social network to another, and from one cultural network to another. Language also varies over time. Language variations from one era to another don't constitute dialects, as described in this chapter, but they are important modifications in the language.

If your local newspaper subscribes to the syndicated column of humorist Dave Barry, then you're familiar with his created persona, "Mr. Language Person," the fictional individual who knows everything there is to know about the English language. As Barry explains, "This [Mr. Language Person] column is the ONLY language column to receive the coveted Lifetime Bathroom Pass from the American Society of University Professors Who Are Never in Their Offices."[27]

Barry provides this description of the creation of the English language: "The English language is a rich verbal tapestry woven together from the tongues of the Greeks, the Angles, the Klaxtons, the Celtics, and many more ancient people, all of whom had severe drinking problems."[28]

If you've ever taught spelling, you may agree with Mr. Language Person!

When the 17th-century colonists arrived in the New World, they brought with them the belongings the passage would allow as well as a language linguists refer to today as Early Modern English (EMnE), the same English used by Milton and Shakespeare.

EMnE did not have a number of words the colonists needed in order to name some of their new experiences in the colonies, consequently there are several Native American **borrowings** we can date back to that time: *hickory, pecan, squash, hominy, suc-cotash, chipmunk, muskrat, raccoon, skunk,* and *woodchuck.*[29]

Furthermore, it is common for immigrants' native language to change, but it changes in ways different from the changes in the home variety. They will continue to use and change the language they bring with them in isolation from the inevitable changes their language will undergo in their home country. The British colonists in North America were, therefore, unaware of the changes that were taking place in EMnE in Great Britain.[30]

This being the case, the 17th-century colonists brought with them in their vocabulary the word *druggist.* In the middle of the 18th century, however, speakers in Great Britain began to use the word *chemist* instead of *druggist.* The older form, *druggist,* from which American English derives the term *drugstore,* still persists in the United States and *chemist* remains today in Great Britain.[31]

Similarly, when the Brits "back home" began to substitute the word *autumn* for the word *fall,* the colonists had no knowledge of this change. Consequently, they continued to use the word *fall,* the predominate term for that particular season that is still used in the United States today. According to Conklin and Laurie, some speakers of BrE consider the use of *fall* in the United States to be archaic.[32]

There were also a number of pronunciation changes taking place in BrE during this same period of time. For example, the colonists brought with them, of course, the pronunciations they had learned and knew, and speakers in the United States today continue to pronounce words like *derby, clerk,* and *Berkeley.* The mid-18th-century BrE speakers were, on the other hand, vowel sounds in these words. More than 250 years later, speakers of BrE render *derby* so that it sounds like *darby, clerk* is pronounced as *clark,* and *Berkeley* is spoken as *Barkley.*[33]

Marking chronological changes in language is like observing changes in humans. It's usually only when we transcend time and take out the family photograph album, attend a high school reunion, or view a home videotape of a family gathering that we notice significant changes.

THE IMPACT OF TELEVISION

One of my students recently suggested that television will, ultimately, "level" regional and social variations in language. His thesis was that as more people watch and listen to the various news commentators, weather reporters, sports analysts, and the like, viewers will, unconsciously, accommodate their language so that it fits the "network standard."

I've heard this thesis before. Although I admire my student's theorizing about language variation, I can't support his theory.

The impact of television and other media on language is a mixed bag. As we have observed before, TV will contribute some trendy phrases to the language, but they seldom have a life beyond popularity ratings.

For example, when *Who Wants to be a Millionaire* was a ratings leader, the host, Regis Philbin, was fond of asking a contestant, "Is this your final answer?" In many social gatherings, as a result, lots of TV watchers would use this phrase, as in "So you think Baywatch University will win the String-Bikini Bowl? Is this your final answer?"

As *Who Wants to Be a Millionaire* fades into TV oblivion, so will "Is this your final answer?" Why is this so? Consider this: If I greeted one of my classes with "Howdy Doody, boys and girls," they would look at me as if I have lobsters growing out of my ears. That greeting was popular in the mid-1950s when Buffalo Bob and Howdy Doody were TV regulars, but today they're not ... and neither is their language. It's archaic.

As for other uses, I accept the notion that TV contributes to dialect standardization or leveling in the area of *vocabulary*, at a macrolevel. Most people understand what's described on television as "a big-screen TV." From watching the television news, they understand what a "summit meeting" is. You can add to this list.

On the other hand, pronunciation variations defy standardization, a point clarified by Dixon.[34] Some groups consciously try to maintain their phonological differences. After observing television, television watchers, and pronunciation patterns, I have noticed few phonological changes over the years. Why do you think this is the case?

SOME NAMING PRACTICES

My friend Joan Rich, a person you've met, is a teacher in an elementary school in our city and has a student this year whose first name is "E-3." This is an unusual first name, but it clearly means something special to the name givers.

Surnames, family names, are usually more predictable. Typically, they're inherited. But, where do our surnames come from?

I'm sure you know someone whose surname is either *Brown*, *Green*, or *White*. On the other hand, I'll wager that you don't know anyone named either *Yellow* or *Magenta*. Why?

The science that studies names and naming practices is known as **onomastics**. This field of study is divided between personal names and geographical place names, although the two are sometimes interchangeable. *Washington*, for example, is both a geographical place name and a common personal name.[35]

Although there is substantial onomastic research reported in the professional literature, you may find a popular novel—Ken Follett's Pillars of the Earth—to be both an informative account of how a number of English surnames began.

Some surnames are derived from the father's name, so that the son of John becomes known as *Johnson*, the son of Robert becomes *Robertson*, and so on. Some family names are derived from geographical features, like *Underhill*, *Forest*, and *Glenn*. Any number of surnames originated from the family's trade or vocation, as in *Barber*, *Carpenter*, *Cook*, *Fletcher*, *Tanner*, *Wheeler*, and the like.[36]

THE LANGUAGES OF RELIGION

There are many excellent books describing the history of phonological, lexical, and grammatical changes in the English language over the past centuries; any college or university library will have many of these books on their shelves. On the other hand, you may have access to a veritable treasure trove of examples of chronological change in either *The Bible* or the hymnal used in your church or home. Because teachers have traditionally been very careful about the separation of church and state, however, these texts have seldom been used in schools in order to note linguistic changes.

It is instructive, for example, to use different editions of Christian *Bibles* and to compare the language found in identical passages. A King James translation of *The Bible*, for example, uses the English language as it was used 400 years ago. *The Good News Bible* or *The Oxford Annotated Bible* use more contemporary English.

Using at least two translations of *The Bible*, look up the answers to the following questions. I'll wager the price of this book that some of the answers will surprise you.

1. How many Wise Men are there in the Christmas story?
2. What fruit did Eve eat and entice Adam to eat in the Garden of Eden?
3. What swallowed Jonah?
4. How many of each kind of animal did Noah take on the Ark?

If your answers to these questions are, respectively, *three, an apple, a whale,* and *two,* you're wrong. For clarification, by question, see (Question 1) Matthew 2:1-12; (Question 2) Genesis 2:15 to Genesis 3:6; (Question 3) Jonah 1:17; and (Question 4) Genesis 7:1-3.[37]

Let's also look at some familiar hymns.[38]

In 1719, Issac Watts first published first published "I'll Praise My Maker While I've Breath." Revised wording was provided by John Wesley in 1737. These dates are important; they remind us that we're looking at English that is 300 years old. In the second verse of this hymn the congregants sing:

Happy are they whose hopes rely on Israel's God,
who made the sky and earth and seas with all their **train**.

Which *train* is it? The A-Train? The Chattanooga Choochoo? Neither, of course. How is *train* being used in this sentence? Your dictionary, if it's a quality dictionary containing **etymologies** (word histories) will help you understand this 300-year-old use of *train.*

In 1907, the American poet Henry Van Dyke wrote words to accompany Beethoven's "Ode to Joy." The result was the now-familiar hymn, "Joyful, Joyful, We Adore Thee." In the third verse of this hymn, people sing:

Thou art giving and forgiving, ever blessing, ever blest,
well-spring of the joy of living, ocean depth of happy rest.

What is a *well-spring*? It must be unconventional English today because my grammar- and spell-checker automatically marked it with a green, squiggley underscore. A well-spring is not a type of mattress you can buy at a department store. As usual, you can clarify the meaning of this older word by looking it up in your dictionary.

Finally, turning to my Welsh heritage, I recall Walter C. Smith's "Immortal, Invisible, God Only Wise" (1867). In the second verse we see the words, "Unresting, **unhasting**, and silent as night ...." What is *unhasting*? You know how to answer that question by now: Check with your dictionary.

THE AGENTS OF LINGUISTIC VARIATION

In Shirley Jackson's short story, "The Lottery," one of the characters complains "Things just ain't the way they used to be." How true this is, in every aspect of life, even beyond the theme of Jackson's portrayal of blind, unthinking tradition.

The agents of linguistic change are the same agents who resist change in Jackson's story: the people. It is a linguistic axiom that when people need to new linguistic form, they'll create one. Similarly, when a form is not longer useful, they'll discard it.

For example, when I was 7 and 8 years of age, blocks of ice were delivered to our home and put in the *ice box*. The term *ice box* was used by everyone on our street because it was the common noun used to name the kitchen appliance where perishable food items were kept.

The term *ice box* has been replaced, as you know, by *refrigerator*.

At the same time my family had an *ice box*, we also had a *record player*, a machine my father used to play his 78-rpm records. Over time, the record player was replaced by a *hi fi*, which was subsequently replaced by a *stereo*. Today, my wife and I use a *CD player*.

As the times and their technologies change, so does our language, as just illustrated. But, let's look at a couple of very old Anglo-Saxon words, *mouse* and *icon*. How these two words are used in the context of computers today is distinctively different from the ways they were used by Geoffrey Chaucer and Robert Burns centuries ago.

Not only do definitions change over time. Pronunciations change, too. Two terms I'm hearing today are the spoken renderings of *realtor* and *nuclear*. I'm hearing these words spoken more a more as *real-a-tor* and as *nuke-you-lar*. How you or I might feel about these changes may be beside the point. These two pronunciations may become "standard" of they are sustained by American English speakers.

The most comprehensive account of English language history is provided by *The Oxford English Dictionary* (OED). Nevertheless, several of the chronological changes in English will be recorded in any reputable collegiate dictionary.

Changes in word meanings are usually described by the following processes:

1. **Elevation**: the meaning of a word has become more elevated, more prestigious. For example, the word *nice* once meant *ignorant*. In earlier times, an *economist* was a *house keeper*. Today, *nice* is better than *ignorant*; an *economist* is more than a *house keeper*.

2. **Degradation**: the opposite of elevation; the meaning of a word has changed from a more positive meaning and has become, over the years, disparaging, negative. A *smirk* was, once, simply a *smile*; today, a smirk is a negative facial expression. Originally, a *gossip* was a *godparent*. Today, a *gossip* is not someone to emulate.

3. **Generalization**: a word with a specific meaning becomes broader, more general. The word *butcher*, for example, once defined a *slayer of goats*. Today a *butcher* prepares all minds of meats.

4. **Specialization**: a word having a broader meaning takes on more limited, more specialized meaning. The word *starve*, for example, was once a synonym for the general infini-

tive, *to die*. Today, of course, *starve* suggests a more specific type of death. Similarly, the word *angel* once meant *messenger*. *Angel* has assumed a more specialized meaning.[39]

BORROWINGS AND IMPOSITIONS

American English users have **borrowed** (see chap. 2) many words from other languages and have incorporated them into the traditional AmE vocabulary. Although a list of examples could go on and on, a few well-chosen words will illustrate just how extensive the borrowing process has been.

From Afrikaans, we have borrowed *veldt*. From Native American languages English has borrowed *totem*, *caucus*, and *raccoon*. *Algebra* and *mattress* come from Arabic, and *tulip* and *yogurt* come from Turkish.[40] Other examples of borrowings are in chapter 2.

Language **imposition**, sometimes referred to as *linguistic imperialism*, can be illustrated easily with regard to the English language with the citation of one date: 1066. One of the most significant moments in the development of the English language took place on this date when William, Duke of Normandy, sometimes referred to as William the Conqueror, defeated the Anglo-Saxons at the Battle of Hastings.

When William the Conqueror defeated the Anglo-Saxons, he did what all conquerors have usually done: He imposed his own sense of political and linguistic reality on his new land and new subjects. For the purposes of this book, we examine only the linguistic impositions.

Serving as the new ruler of the country known today as Great Britain, William, Duke of Normandy, exercised his "to the victor belong the spoils" prerogatives. As he redefined local government, he named his supporters, all Norman French, of course, to positions of leadership.

As a consequence of these appointments, the language of William's appointees—the French language—became the "official" language of the church, the courts, the schools, and "high" society. Thus, a new language, the language of power, prestige, and position, was imposed on the Anglo-Saxons.

Although a discussion of the impact of this imposition could go on for several chapters, I'll stop here with just a couple of notes.

Note 1: Some 950 years later, almost a century, the more prestigious words in the English vocabulary are derived from *French* words. Consider, for example, the following comparisons; the Anglo-Saxon word is enclosed in quotation marks and the words derived from French is in italics. Which word is more prestigious, "loving" or *amorous*, "cow" or *beef*, "deep" or *profound*, "sharp" or *poignant*, "hut" or *cottage*?

Note 2: As I write this book, if speakers or writers want to demonstrate that they possess any degree of *savoir faire*, they will do so by inserting a French expression into their discourse.

LANGUAGE REGISTERS

Often the activity in which one is engaged helps to shape the language choices one makes. As a university professor, in any given semester I might teach one class with 50 students, another with 25, and a graduate-level seminar with 7 to 10 students. I offer academic and career advice to my advisees, and I attend department and college faculty meetings. I also talk to numerous teachers in K–12 classrooms and workshops. As I move from one context to another, my language choices will vary.

I am neither special nor unique. Think about all of the conversational contexts you've been a part of during the past 4 or 5 days. Your language choices have reflected the same types of social and professional, formal and informal settings. These setting have influenced your language choices, too.

Linguistically distinct activities are usually called **genres** or **registers**.[41]

We examined one aspect of registers earlier: You'll recall that people who speak *with* one another speak *like* one another. This is true for both regional and social dialects; it is also true for people in the same vocation. Teachers talk like other teachers, physicians usually talk like other physicians, and so on.

Language registers are not based solely on occupational similarities. Our hobbies will also help to shape some language choices. When I'm fishing with Neighbor Norman, we say things like *Good cast, Keep your line taut,* and *It's a keeper.* These expressions are clearly within the fishing register, but not in the quilting, swimming, or stamp collecting registers.

You've learned many registers during your life, and you've learned, as well, how to shift from one register to another when the context requires a shift.

A good example of the ease and rapidity of register-shifting was recently provided by my wife.

Suffering from a painful bone spur on her left heel, my wife went to a podiatrist, seeking relief from the pain. Both my wife and the podiatrist are African-American females, an important fact, as you'll see.

Using her professional physician's register, the podiatrist began with predictable, medically appropriate inquiries, asking my wife about when the pain occurs, under what conditions, with what kinds of footwear, and so on. Toward the end of the examination, the podiatrist asked my wife to walk from one end of the examination room to the other.

After observing my wife's gait, the podiatrist suddenly switched registers and said, "Girl, I can't tell which crazy way you walkin'."

The podiatrist judiciously offered her professional solution to the bone spur problem, then the two of them spent the rest of their time talking "sister talk" about some things Black women talk about in a predominately White community: Where do you get your hair done? Where do you buy your cosmetics?

Quicker than it takes to describe, they shifted registers easily and quickly.

LANGUAGE CHANGE, VARIATION, AND ATTITUDES

Dixon described how a language can undergo major changes when the linguistic equilibrium in a speech community is punctuated by a cataclysmic event. The punctuation might be an act of nature, like a major drought or volcanic eruption; or, it might be due to the emergence of an aggressive political or religious group; or, it might be due to a striking technological innovation.[42]

William the Conqueror's victory at the Battle of Hastings is an example of Dixon's punctuated equilibrium thesis.

This does not mean, however, that even during periods of equilibrium that the political, economic, technological, or linguistics contexts remain stable. They don't. There are constant linguistic alterations taking place, a perpetual ebb and flow of language change.[43]

For example, you read in chapter 2 about the various ways new English words can be created. **Coinages**, the results of fertile minds, are truly "new" words that haven't existed before. Examine the over-the-counter medicines you can purchase today for upset stomachs. *Pepcid* and *Zantac*, either as products or as words, didn't exist just a few years ago. This is an example of language change.

Another example is the use of terms that society considers "in" words. The use of *Y2K* as an acronym for the "year 2000" is an example. I saw *Y2K* plastered all over newspapers, magazines, and advertising circulars. It became a buzz word in many conversations, as did the word *millennium*.

Advertisers were quick to jump on the commercial possibilities of using *millennium* in connection with the sales of liquor, fireworks, clothes, home appliances, and just about any other goods and services the purchasing public might want or need. In time, these buzz words are replaced; they usually have a short shelf life.

Other changes have a longer life and a more lasting effect on the language. Because of changes in people and their attitudes, some words commonly used today were frowned on just 25 years ago. In the recent past, for example, no one spoke openly using the word *condom*. Today, the word *condom* is used with ease by many, it's heard on radio and television programs, and *condoms* are displayed next to the chewing gum on a display rack at one bookstore on my campus.

A recent letter-writer to the "Word Court" column in *The Atlantic Monthly* calls the expression *How can I help you?* the most ubiquitous linguistic error in English-speaking North America. The author of the letter prefers *How may I help you?*[44]

Any one of these changes may not bother you. Some are troublesome to other English speaker-writers. Jean Aitchison captured the essence of attitudes toward language change in her appropriately titled book, *Language Change: Progress or Decay?*[45]

Whether you view language changes as progress or decay, I can guarantee that changes will continue. You and I may or may not like the changes, but they are part of language's perpetual ebb and flow.

FOR DISCUSSION

Directions: Based on what you now and what you have read in this chapter, how will you answer the following questions?

1. How are *accent* and *dialect* different?
2. List the forces that contributed to the shaping of your idiolect. Which ones were stronger? Which were evident, but weaker?
3. Is it possible to maintain the status quo in anything?
4. What makes Standard American English *standard*?
5. How are *regional* and *social* dialects similar?
6. In your view, which dialect feature—lexical, phonological, or grammatical—has the greatest potential for social stigmatization?
7. Explain the relationship between *culture* and *language*.
8. Explain the Etymological Fallacy, with examples.
9. What changes faster, a spelling or a pronunciation? Why?
10. How does necessity promote invention?

NOTES

1. Tom McArthur, ed., *The Oxford Companion to the English Language* (Oxford, UK: Oxford University Press, 1992), 982.
2. Roy Harris, *The Language Myth* (London: Duckworth, 1981), 10.
3. Ann Ruggles Gere and Eugene Smith, *Attitudes, Language and Change* (Urbana, IL: National Council of Teachers of English, 1979), 8–10.

4. Nancy Faires Conklin and Margaret A. Lourie, *A Host of Tongues: Language Communities in the United States* (New York: Macmillan–The Free Press, 1983), 23.
5. Ibid.
6. Margaret Wade-Lewis, "The Status of Semantic Items from African Languages in American English," *The Black Scholar* (Vol. 23, No. 26, Summer 1993), 26.
7. Robert Hendrickson, *American Talk: The Words and Ways of American Dialects* (New York: Penguin Books, 1996), 132–133.
8. David Crystal, *The Cambridge Encyclopedia of Language*, 2nd ed. (Cambridge, England: Cambridge University Press, 1997), 35.
9. Monica Crabtree and Joyce Powers, *Language Files*, 5th ed. (Columbus: Ohio State University Press, 1991), 381.
10. Edward Finegan and Niko Besnier, *Language: Its Structure and Use* (New York: Harcourt Brace Jovonovich, 1989), 383.
11. Marko Modiano, "Standard English(es) and Educational Practices for the World's Lingua Franca," *English Today* (Vol. 15, No. 4, October 1999), 8.
12. Ibid.
13. For example, see Frederick G. Cassidy (ed.), *Dictionary of American Regional English* (Cambridge, MA: Belknap Press of the Harvard University Press, 1985); Craig M. Carver, *American Regional Dialects* (Ann Arbor: University of Michigan Press, 1949). There are additional references by Kurath and Kurath and McDavid available in any research library.
14. Finegan and Besnier, ibid.
15. Robert M. W. Dixon, *The Rise and Fall of Languages* (Cambridge, England: Cambridge University Press, 1997), 19.
16. Cited in Jeff Siegel, "Stigmatized and Standardized Varieties in the Classroom: Interference or Separation?", *TESOL Quarterly* (Vol. 33, No. 4, Winter 1999), 702.
17. Ibid., 710
18. Ibid.
19. Ibid., 721.
20. Roger Lass, *Historical Linguistics and Language* Change (Cambridge, England: Cambridge University Press, 1998), xv.

21. William Labov, *The Social Stratification of English in New York City* (Washington, DC: The Center for Applied Linguistics, 1996).

22. Peter Trudgill, *Accent, Dialect, and the School* (London: Edward Arnold, 1975), 35.

23. Conklin and Laurie, 115

24. Ibid.

25. Crystal, 23.

26. Dilin Liu and Bryan Farha, "Three Strikes and You're Out," *English Today* (Vol. 12, No. 1, January 1996), 36.

27. Dave Barry, "Mr. Language Person Finds His Nitch," *Lincoln* (NE) *Journal Star*, December 5, 1999.

28. Cited in Steven Pinker, *The Language Instinct* (New York: Morrow, 1994), 246.

29. Conklin and Laurie, 75–76.

30. Ibid., 76.

31. Ibid.

32. Ibid.

33. Ibid.

34. Dixon, 106

35. Crystal, 112.

36. "Q & A," *The Atlantic Monthly* (Vol. 270, No. 4, October 1992), 14.

37. I am indebted to Terry Cain, my friend, former pastor, and mentor for this activity.

38. All of the hymn citations are taken from *The United Methodist Hymnal* (Nashville, TN: The United Methodist Publishing House, 1989).

39. Monica Crabtree and Joyce Powers, *Language Files* (5th ed., Columbus: Ohio State University Press, 1991), 327.

40. Hendrickson, chapter 1.

41. Crystal, 52.

42. Dixon, 67.

43. Ibid., 69.

44. Barbara Wallraff, "Word Court," *The Atlantic Monthly* (Vol. 285, No. 1, January 2000), 132.

45. Jean Aitchison, *Language Change: Progress or Decay?* (New York: Universe Books, 1985).

CHAPTER 6

Meaning and Signification

But let's not forget that a word hasn't got a meaning given to it, as it were, by a power independent of us, so that there could be a kind of scientific investigation into what the word really means. A word has the meaning someone has given to it.

—Ludwig Wittgenstein, *The Blue Book*

As you approach this chapter, please consider these questions. How *tall* is a tall building or a tall person? How tall must the building or person be before we can use the adjective *tall*? Can a *tall* building in one city be a *short* building when compared to a building in another city? Can a *tall* person be a *short* person in another context? What does *tall* "mean" and how did you learn this?

118

Sean Green is a former student in one of my language classes. One night he shared with the class an experience he had while escorting six visiting students from another country to Kansas City. As he was driving the university van along a major thoroughfare, another driver cut sharply in front of Sean, causing him to use all of his defensive driving skills. "Really nice," Sean sarcastically muttered.

"What was 'nice' about that," one of the visiting students asked? "I don't think it was 'nice'."

"You're right," Sean replied, "it wasn't 'nice'. It was bad ... and stupid."

"Then why did you say 'nice'?"

Sean went on to describe a lengthy conversation he had with the student about the possible meanings of *nice*, and how the meanings of words can be shaped by the context and the speaker's intent. The visiting student had learned only one sense of *nice*, and Sean had lots of explaining to do.

Students for whom English is a new language are often confounded by the almost infinite number of ways English words can be used by native speakers, sometimes, as with *nice*, completely reversing the conventional sense of a word.

As the Wittgenstein quote at the beginning of this chapter suggests, an English word does not have a fixed, immutable meaning. Almost any English word can be invested with an unconventional use and meaning, depending upon how the word is used in a sentence in a particular context.[1]

Meaning, a word like many other words we use frequently, is sometimes difficult to define because people are extremely inventive with language and they can mean many things with one word. Indeed, in their early and important book, *The Meaning of Meaning* (1923) C. K. Ogden and I. A. Richards provide 16 different meanings for the words **mean** and **meaning**. Here's just a sample:[2]

John *means* to write. ("intends")
A green light *means* go. ("indicates")
Health *means* everything. ("has importance")
His look was full of *meaning*. ("special import")

What is the *meaning* of life? ("point," "purpose")
What does "capitalist" *mean* to you? ("convey")
What does cornea *mean*? ("refer to in the world")

As a professional observer of language and how people use it, I have tentatively concluded that we use a lot of words with only casual regard, until a particular use of a certain word strikes us as either especially appropriate, not appropriate at all, beautiful, or downright crazy. When someone hits one of our linguistic hot buttons, then we react to a word's use.

For example, one of the largest high schools in my state recently changed the name of its athletic teams from *The Indians* to *The Patriots*.

Several leaders in the Native American community objected to the use of *The Indians*; the use of this term, they said, is demeaning to their people and dehumanizes them, turning them into stereotyped "savages" most often seen in Grade-B movies.

Not so, defenders of *The Indians* replied. The original name was intended to evoke connotations of skill, intelligence, loyalty, and courage.

This word war, conducted in the press and on radio and television stations, was settled when *The Patriots* was selected as the new athletic name. Whether the success of this school's athletic teams in their respective arenas of endeavor will be enhanced or endangered as a result of the name change remains to be seen.

The same conflict is being waged between Native Americans and other athletic teams, at both the high school and professional levels. The issue of team names might not be important to you, or you may be enraged; as you can appreciate, I have no way of knowing your political or social predispositions.

My purpose in introducing the athletic team controversy is simply to demonstrate how a *name* can engender strongly felt emotions, the result of hitting linguistic hot buttons.

While we're on the topic of athletic team names, recall with me the names of some teams you may know, the *Storm*, the *Cyclones*, the *Giants*, the *Bears*. What do these names convey to you? If you're a fan of one of these teams, the name *means* a lot. If you're not, the name *means* little.

I'll bet you the cost of a seven-course dinner at your favorite restaurant, however, that you will never hear about a bonafide athletic team named the *Dwarfs*, the *Grass*, or the *Box Springs and Mattress*. Why? The answer, I think, is simple: word magic.

In almost every corner of the world, we can observe the magical powers of language. The conviction that words can exercise control over spirits, events, people, and things is demonstrated routinely through the uses of magical formulae, magical expressions and responses, litanies of names, and in organized religion.[3]

For example, in some cultures, when a person sneezes someone in the group will say either *Gesundheit* ("health") or *Bless you*. These formulaic sayings have traditionally been used to deflect illness. In many religious ceremonies, the formal service begins with an invocation and ends with a benediction; both of these liturgical elements summon a higher spirit's blessing on the congregation. At sporting events, cheerleaders orchestrate special incantations and lead the audience in the singing of "fight" songs, and everyone believes these activities will magically inspire the team.

Words have a mystical quality with place names, as well. New nations, for example, usually change their names when they achieve independence. In Africa, according to one of my doctoral students, Doreen Moyo who is from Zimbabwe, *Rhodesia* was renamed as *Zimbabwe*, and its capital city's name was changed from *Salisbury* to *Harare*. Similarly, the former nation of *Dahomey* became *Benin*, *French Sudan* became *Mali*, and *Gold Coast* became *Ghana*.

The new names symbolize a new, independent, and sovereign people.

On Sunday mornings while I'm showering and dressing, I tune in one of the "talking heads" television programs in order to learn more about the political scene. Whether the guests are campaigning for office or attacking, defending, or promoting pending legislation, they habitually rely on words with mystical, magical, built-in judgments.

As you can appreciate, it is as difficult to define *reasonable, prosperity, liberal, conservative, family values,* and *traditional val-*

ues as it is to define *tall*. Nevertheless, these words are used with extraordinary regularity.

The language of advertising uses different types of word magic. Clearly, an advertising agency has a single mission: to bring attention to its clients' products, goods, and services, so effectively that the purchasing public will buy what the client has to offer.

Consequently, the language used is typically emphatic and flattering, and there are grammatical constructions which look and sound like the final and absolute truth is being reported: *Widgerderm cleans faster and better*. Faster and better than what? *Widgerderm costs less*. Less than what? *People are saying Widgerderm is the best*. Who are these people?

The names of cars are carefully selected in order to connote good taste and luxury, or frugality and economy. In my morning newspaper, the following automobiles are offered: *Regal, Park Avenue, Monte Carlo,* and *Grand Marquis*. Some antonyms—*Unimposing, Maple Street, Osage Beach,* and *Commoner*—aren't likely candidates; they just don't conjure up the right kind of word magic.

For similar reasons, no line of cruise ships will likely christen a new ship with the name *Titanic*. Or, it's why farmers and ranchers raise *sheep* and *cattle*, but on a menu they're called *lamb* and *beef*.

Words and other symbols have at least two separate but related senses, or "meanings." Many words and symbols carry "external" meanings. For example, the printed symbols $, %, @, and ? have been invested with general meanings by the people who grew up in the culture using these typographical symbols. Their general "meanings" are external to the user, part of the social facts of the user's culture. Similarly, other symbols that are used in other cultures—like β or £—may not evoke much of a response from some native English speakers.

Many words and symbols may also have "inner" senses, or meanings. The "inner" senses reside within the mind of the user. When Sean Green used the word *nice* in a sarcastic manner, he was invoking an "inner" sense of the word, a sense that seemed reasonable to him at the time and under the circumstances. His "inner" meaning, however, was in conflict with the visiting student's "external," or conventional understanding of the word.

Similarly, the place name I used earlier, *Osage Beach*, refers to a municipality in southern Missouri; the external meaning denotes the name of a town; *Osage Beach* also has an inner meaning for me, because the hearing or reading of this place name reminds me of many happy vacation days in the Missouri Ozarks. If you aren't familiar with Osage Beach, then you're likely to relate to this term only at the external meaning level.

Here is a letter to the editor of my local newspaper further illustrating the uses of "external" and "inner" meanings:

> Two weeks ago my mother, daughter and I were in Lincoln for some meetings and were fortunate enough to take in several Star City holiday festival activities, including the December 5 parade. While the parade was enjoyable for all three generations, I remain disturbed by one thing. As the color guard rounded the corner, only a handful of people stood for the passing of the flag. Among those already standing, only a few paused to salute. As my mother and I rose and I placed my two-year-old's hand over her heart, I inquired of those around me, "Isn't anyone going to stand and salute the flag?" The puzzled looks from parents and children were shocking. I felt sorry for the veterans bearing the flag passing by. Since I am not from Lincoln, I am curious. Do the elementary school children receive any lessons in flag etiquette? Do the parents share in the processes if there are? Standing to salute is such a simple thing and it has a tremendous heritage behind it. No wonder our society is in such turmoil if even the simplest acts of civility are starting to fall by the wayside.[4]

We can only use the text available to us because you and I weren't there, so there are several questions remaining about this report. For one, is this an accurate report of what actually happened? Furthermore, only "a handful of people" stood up when the flag passed by the spectators. How many is a "handful?" Two? Twenty-two? I assume the flag referred to is the U.S. flag, but could it be the state flag?

I am not demeaning the writer with my questions (and there are others we could ask); I am simply posing questions I think any reader might ask. I do know this: the writer is bothered that more spectators didn't stand, that they didn't salute the flag, that the flag-bearers were treated dishonorably, that some spectators don't appreciate the heritage undergirding the flag, and the writer believes that ignoring simple acts of civility are creating turmoil in society.

Let's assume the report is accurate. More people remained seated, apparently, when the flag passed by. Those spectators who grew up in this culture recognize the U.S. flag as a commonly viewed symbol, an "external" meaning.

The writer of the letter, however, not only recognizes the "external" meanings associated with the U.S. flag, but the writer is also investing additional "inner" meanings: the flag has a heritage; veterans who have defended the flag deserve recognition; flag etiquette is important; attending to flag etiquette and other acts of civility prevent social dysfunction.

We may have visited this letter longer than you'd prefer, so let me close with this brief summary. Not everyone invests the same degree of meaning to symbols or symbolic acts.

The different degrees of meaning attached to symbols and symbolic acts can be observed at almost any ceremony. When athletic contests begin with the singing of the national anthem, not everyone joins in with the same amount of attentiveness or vigor. When church groups read a collect or responsive reading, some congregants will enter into this activity with more solemnity than others. When civic organizations recite "The Pledge of Allegiance" to the flag, some members of the club fully enter into the recitation, while others may be reading the agenda, peeking out the window to check on the weather, examining their appointment books, or flicking lint off a neighbor's sleeve.

Degrees of invested meaning, both external and, especially, inner, vary from person to person.

Be a linguist. How many different words can you think of to refer to the following?

bathroom	drunk	fat	janitor	stupid
old person	death	pregnant		corpse

Why do we use these different words?

GENERAL SEMANTICS

The linguistic field of study broadly called *semantics* can be subdivided into more specialized areas like how meaning is structured in language (componential analysis, lexical field, semantic features); the relationships among words, people, things, and events in the world (reference, signs, semiotics); and different types of meaning (connotation, denotation).

Before your eyes glaze over with the length of this list, bear with me, please: We are not going to discuss each of these fields of inquiry in detail. I am simply trying to illustrate how complex the study of semantics can be.

We'll discuss in this section of the book only the rudiments of general semantics, primarily as a foundation.

The word **semantics** is derived from the Greek words *semantikos* ("significant") and *semainein* ("to signify," "to mean"). The early general semanticists, consequently, studied the relationships between and among people, things, events, and the names people used to describe those relationships and corresponding meanings.

The field of general semantics was introduced to readers in the United States by Alfred Korzybski, author of *Science & Sanity: An Introduction to Non-Aristotelian Systems and General Semantics*. Korzybski's book, very arduous reading, in my view, attracted the attention of several U.S. scholars, like S. I. Hayakawa, Stuart Chase, Wendell Chase, and Irving Lee; through their reading of Korzybski and their own scholarship, they helped to interpret Korzybski's ideas.

During the 1940s and 1950s the general semantics movement blossomed in the United States, primarily because of Korzybski's intellectual influence on S. I. Hayakawa and Alan Hayakawa's book *Language in Action*.

Consider the historical context. In the 1940s the United States and its allies were astonished at the successes of Hitler and Mussolini in manipulating language ("the big lie") and, consequently, people, in order to achieve their political and military objectives.

Hayakawa was one of those who helped readers examine language in a new way. Interest in general semantics was very keen inasmuch as this relatively new field of study might help, readers believed, to understand international distortions in language and thought. As a matter of fact, Hayakawa's *Language in Action* was selected by the Book-of-the-Month Club as its December 1941 offering.[5] This is a monumental achievement for a book about language study.

In the late 1950s, however, the field of linguistics experienced a profound paradigm shift.

Noam Chomsky's *Syntactic Structures*, published in 1957, described transformational-generative grammar, which de-emphasized semantics.[6]

Chomsky's propositions in *Syntactic Structures* placed him at the center of language study and his influence on the linguistics community remains strong today. I've attended meetings of professional societies devoted to the study of languages in the United States, Great Britain, Canada, and Scotland, and it's not at all uncommon to hear some professional linguists identify and define themselves with comments like "Please understand, I'm Chomskyean." or "My views are definitely non-Chomskyean."

Thus, interest in semantics and meaning, especially in the United States, diminished, momentarily. Attention to meaning was revived, however, largely through the combined efforts of reading educators, psychologists, and linguists. Because a number of Korzybski's propositions are useful in a consideration of meaning and how it is constructed, a review of some of them will be beneficial.

SOME OF KORZYBSKI'S CONTRIBUTIONS

Alfred Korzybski was a renaissance man: a professional engineer, a philosopher, a mathematician, and an amateur linguist. (Please note, I do not use *amateur* as a disparaging term. The word *amateur* comes to English from the Latin verb *amare*, meaning "to love." Consequently, an *amateur* is one who engages in an activity for the love of it.). With the publication of *Science & Sanity* in 1933, Korzybski established the field of general semantics. Some of the principles he established are discussed here.

Meaning Is Not in Words, But in People. A word's meaning is not transmitted either from a symbol on a page of text to a reader or from a speaker's mouth to a listener, Korzybski suggested. Rather, people attach or ascribe meaning to a word. We don't *get*, but we *give* meanings to words.[7]

For example, if you encounter the word *we:nag*, from the Tohono O'odham (Papago) language, or the word *otooto* from Japanese, you'll probably not be able to "get" any meaning from these words simply by looking at them; the meaning doesn't jump from the page to you. The words don't "tell" you anything.

If, on the other hand, the reader-listener has encountered either of these words before and has potential meanings for them stored in his or her long- or short-term memory, then the reader-listener will likely access the appropriate memory and ascribe the suitable meanings to the words.

Words Are Not What They Refer To. Another way of saying this is: "The word is not the thing." Korzybski pointed out that an object, an event, a thing, a person, an idea, or a feeling is *unspeakable*. We can name, define, and describe objects, events, things, persons, ideas, and feelings, but in using language for the naming, defining, or describing, we haven't "said" the object, event, etc. An upset stomach, for example, might be expressed or described in words, but the expression or description isn't the same things as the condition of "upset stomach." The condition is unspeakable; it simply exists.[8]

Words are usually symbols for objects, events, persons, and so on, but they are always arbitrary abstractions. Because they are abstractions, they are removed from the level of total objectivity, which is always *unspeakable*.[9]

So, when we say a word, we haven't actually said the "thing" the word refers to. If you say that you're "happy," you've named an emotional state but the condition *itself* hasn't been spoken. If you say you're "tired," you're describing your physical condition, but the physical circumstance *itself* hasn't been spoken, it's simply there.

There are at least three fascinating aspects of this principle.

First, please recall our earlier discussion about how language is **arbitrary**. We might see, for example, an animal and, in American English, appropriately call the animal a *pig*. We haven't "said" the animal, mind you, we've merely named it. In other cultures, however, where different languages are used, that same critter might be named a *cerdo*, a *schwein*, or a *cochon*.

It matters not which language is being used in naming the vertebrate, four-legged mammals that have stout bodies, short legs, thick and usually bristled skins, long snouts, and short tails; the speaker still hasn't "said" the animal.

Second, confusing a word with the word's unspeakable referent sometimes results in the use of **euphemisms**. Children are cautioned, for example, to avoid using taboo words, often because the taboo words are "dirty." Confusing the word with the thing the word refers to, some parents implicitly understand that if the word is in the child's mouth, it's the same thing as having the "dirty" thing in the mouth. Consequently, an age-old punishment for using "dirty" words is to wash the child's mouth with soap. You see this scene re-enacted every December when several TV channels televise Jean Shepard's *A Christmas Story*.

To avoid taboo or indelicate words and phrases, people often turn to euphemisms. Euphemisms allow people to go to either the *bathroom*, the *powder room*, or the *restroom*, even when they have no intention of taking either a bath, a powder, or a rest.

We consider euphemisms in more detail later in this chapter.

Third, people attach or ascribe different meanings to the same or related concepts expressed by words. For example, if you're a pet fancier and either own a dog or once owned a dog, the word *dog* is likely to convey to you happy memories and thoughts; in the U.S. culture, dog is man's best friend. Dogs are loyal, true, and faithful. In the Middle East, on the other hand, dogs are never domesticated. Dogs are wild creatures to be avoided at all costs. People from Middle Eastern cultures cannot understand why so many U.S. residences are homes for dogs and their masters.

Language Operates on Varying Levels of Abstraction.
Korzybski pointed out that language can be very general and abstract at one end of a continuum, or it can be quite specific and concrete at the other end.[10]

More abstract language is removed from a verifiable referent. For example, if I tell you that I'm going to the mall to shop for some new clothes, you really haven't learned much. You don't know whether I'm shopping or a new business suit, a new dress shirt, new socks, new tee shirts, or new tennis shorts. In this example, *new clothes* lacks a verifiable referent.

On the other hand, if I tell you I'm going to the mall to buy a new pair of Gold-toe, over-the calf socks, size 9, then my language is much more concrete. There's a verifiable referent.

Using my initial phrase, *new clothes*, examine the following sentences. You'll notice that the sentences move progressively from the most abstract to the most concrete.

1. I'm shopping for new clothes.
2. I'm shopping for a new pair of pants.
3. I'm shopping for a new pair of casual pants.
4. I'm shopping for a new pair of casual pants for fishing.
5. I'm shopping for a new pair of Levis, regular cut, size 33–30.

Sentence 1 is very abstract; as we've already observed. This sentence has no verifiable referent and, therefore, refers to anything and, consequently, nothing. Sentence 5, on the other hand, is about as concrete as it could be. There's a specific referent in this sentence; there is no "range of potential understanding" in this sentence. You know exactly and precisely to what the sentence refers.

As already discussed, the language of advertising can be very abstract. The latest issue of one of my fishing magazines arrived yesterday, and one of the full-page display ads claims that "The nation's top pros recommend Pro-Tech." Who are they? Another ad begins, "The best things in life are Basic." What are "the best things in life?" Might these "best things" vary from person to person?

Political candidates often thrive on vague, abstract language. In the last general election in my state, both the Republican and the Democratic candidate included "Nebraska values" in his campaign ads on television. What are these values? Are they the same on the Native American reservation in Macy, Nebraska, as they are in inner-city Omaha?

One of the greatest challenges teachers face in their classrooms is to help learners who are linguistic apprentices learn how to use more precise language. Every middle school teacher on the planet has no doubt heard, "I don't like this book. It's dumb!" Or, the opposite: "I love this book. It's neat." Why? Can you be more specific?

Meaning Has Direction. If you'll recall our earlier discussion of "external" and "internal" meanings, or if you're already familiar with the terms *denotation* and *connotation*, then you already understand this observation from Korzybski. He used different terminology, however. Meaning, as Korzybski described its direction, can be either **intensional** (connotation) or **extensional** (denotation).

Some helpful distinctions between intensional and extensional language have been provided by one of Korzybski's former students. The extensional meaning of an utterance is that "thing" the utterance refers to in the real world. The extensional meaning is best provided by pointing to the "thing," whether it's a car, a lamp, a hat, or a book.[11]

Those trying to communicate with each other, however, can't always point to the meanings they intend, whether the "thing" is a physical object, an emotion, or an idea. This is why the more familiar term *denotation* is useful.

For example, earlier in this book I have mentioned my neighbor Norman Magruder, my friend who frequently goes fishing with me. I could not explain the "meaning" of Norman Magruder by pointing to him, thereby expressing an extensional meaning. However, you are familiar with words in American English like *neighbor, friend,* and *fishing*. These words denote, signify, and represent concepts you know, so you easily understood what I was saying.[12]

Intensional meanings, on the other hand, are less verifiable and less objective. Intensional meanings are those subjective connotations we ascribe to many words. As you know, some words evoke positive feelings, whereas other words conjure up negative feelings.[13]

Why, do you suppose, a product like *Lean Cuisine* wasn't named *Food Low in Fat*? What's the difference between *celebration* and *observation*? What's the difference between *veal* and *baby beef*? Do you enjoy hearing *information* or *rumor*? To these words and thousands more, we attach either positive or negative shades of meanings; they are called intensional meanings, or connotations.

Usually, the words we use have both extensional and intensional meanings, although one type of meaning may be more dominant. For example, the symbol © denotes "copyright." You're not likely to attach any emotional significance (connotation) to this symbol, although it's possible someone might. Similarly, the symbol denotes "does not equal." Again, it is doubtful that many people will ascribe positive or negative connotations to this symbol.

Conversely, a product claims in its advertising that it's "slightly ahead of our time." This expression has no verifiable, extensional meaning, but it's brimful of positive, attractive, and attracting connotations.

Identification. Identification, as Korzybski described it, is a "semantic disturbance" consisting of errors in meanings.[14]

As I understand Korzybski, *identification* is the term he used to describe the process of treating all instances or cases of a particular phenomenon as *identical*. Consequently, the "semantic disturbance" of identification is at work when a person does not distinguish one "thing" from the family it belongs to. Thus all Democrats are alike; all Republicans are alike; all teenagers, school teachers, African Americans, Jews, Baptists, "jocks," women drivers; mothers-in-law, and so on.

If Korzybski were writing *Science & Sanity* today, I suspect he might use the term **stereotyping** instead of the term **identification**.

Identification certainly makes the world a simpler place, but it's disturbing and inaccurate. *All* African Americans aren't natural athletes anymore than *all* Jews are shrewd business people or *all* mothers-in-law are nosy or *all* "jocks" are dumb.

Korzybski's suggested solution for this "semantic disturbance" was the use of index numbers (superscripts), so that

African American 1 can be distinguished from African American 2, Jew 1 from Jew 2, mother-in-law 1 from mother-in-law 2, and so on.

This suggestion may seem impractical to you. "How in the world," you might ask, "can I stick an index number on every person, place, thing, or idea I talk or write about?" Your point is well taken, but given the domineering tone of Korzybski's prose, I rather suspect he fully expected everyone to follow his advice. My advice is: Be practical and *think* indexing. You'll avoid "semantic disturbances" if you do. Indexing helps us to avoid stereotyping.

EUPHEMISMS

An **euphemism** has been defined as an auspicious or more exalted term that is used instead of a more down-to-earth term.[15] An euphemism for "garbage collector," given this definition, might be "sanitation engineer." A goodly number of students prefer to describe themselves in the written work they submit as "learning facilitators" rather than as "teachers." Some automobile dealers advertise "pre-owned" or "experienced" cars, but not "used" cars. A clothing store in my city invites readers of its newspaper ads to visit one of its "suit brokers" rather than "sales clerks."

The self-appointed language critics we have mentioned earlier frequently cite the use of euphemisms as a deceitful practice, employed by those who have something either to hide or an uglier reality to avoid. Frankly, I don't know that the use of euphemisms is necessarily all that bad, but you'll be your own judge.

I think we need to decide why the euphemism is used before we pass judgment.

Several years ago the name of the U.S. War Department was changed to the Department of Defense. Why? Some advertisements refer to "nervous wetness" rather than "sweat." Why? When did "soap operas" become "daytime dramas?" Why? When did "undertakers" become "morticians?" Can you think of alternative terms for "shortfall," "full-figured," "plus-sized," or "facial blemishes?"

Sometimes, however, we use euphemisms because we're trying to be sensitive to others. Using "passed away" or "passed" for "died" isn't necessarily an attempt to be deceitful or to hide or mask reality. We may use these terms because we're sensitive to the needs of a family that has recently experienced a death of a loved one.[16]

You might apply this simple analysis against language you suspect to be euphemizing:[17]

1. Who is saying what to whom,
2. under what circumstances,
3. under what conditions,
4. with what intent, and
5. with what results?

If you and I were having a cup of coffee or tea right now, we'd return to chapter 4 and consider the uses of discourse conventions and how they contribute to the semantic meaning of our interactions with others. But, because we're not, you'll need to complete the comparisons between chapter 4 and this chapter on your own.

Meaning can be an elusive concept, but it's one we must consider because meaning is the aspect of language people are most often attracted to. In everyday conversations, I've never heard anyone ask, "Why did you begin that last sentence with a gerund?" On the other hand, I've heard people say, with great regularity, "What did you mean by that?"

As early as 1933, Korzybski understood the importance of the power of language when he wrote:

> Man's achievements rest upon the use of symbols. For this reason, we must consider ourselves as a symbolic, semantic class of life, and those who rule the symbols, rule us.[18]

Those who are learning English as a new language understand, perhaps only intuitively, what Korzybski was talking about. They are in your classroom to learn a new language and a new culture. The language barrier is, at first, seemingly insurmountable; some ENL learners feel lost, incapacitated, and powerless. As they progress in their English proficiency, however, most of these feelings will go away and they'll realize the benefits and the promise of having greater options available to them.

FOR DISCUSSION

Directions: Based on what you know and what you have read in this chapter, how will you answer the following questions?

1. Why do some words trigger automatic responses?
2. How can euphemisms contribute to "semantic disturbances?"
3. How can words simultaneously have intensional and extensional meanings?
4. Is meaning influenced by the reader-listener's emotional state?
5. What's the difference between a blueprint and a house?
6. Are taboo words more or less abstract?
7. How are "the power of discourse" and "the discourse of power" related?
8. How are language beliefs different from language knowledge?
9. How tall is a tall building, and how do you know?
10. What are culture-bound symbols?

NOTES

1. Ludwig Wittgenstein, *The Blue and Brown Books* (New York: Harper Torchbooks, 1960), 28.
2. Cited in David Crystal, *The Cambridge Encyclopedia of Language* (2nd ed., Cambridge, England: Cambridge University Press, 1997), 1900.
3. Ibid., 8
4. Letter to the editor, *Lincoln* (NE) *Journal Star*, December 18, 1992, 16.
5. Peter Hasserlriis, "From Pearl Harbor to Watergate to Kuwait: Language in Thought and Action," *English Journal* (Vol. 80, No. 2, 1991), 28.
6. Ross Evans Paulson, *Language, Science, and Action: Korzybski's General Semantics: A Study in Comparative Intellectual History* (Westport, CT: Greenwood Press, 1983), 87.

7. Alfred Korzybski, Alfred, *Science and Sanity: An Introduction to Non-Aristotelian Systems and General Semantics* (4th ed., Lakeville, CT: International Non-Aristotelian Publishing, 1958), 21–22.
8. Ibid., 34.
9. Ibid., 92.
10. Ibid., 389.
11. S. I. Hayakawa and Alan R. Hayakawa, *Language in Thought and Action* (5th ed., New York: Harcourt Brace, 1990), 36.
12. Ibid., 36–37.
13. Ibid., 37.
14. Korzybski, 452.
15. Neil Postman, *Crazy Talk, Stupid Talk* (New York: Delacorte Press, 1976), 208.
16. Ibid., 22
17. William Lutz, "Notes Toward a Definition of Doublespeak," in William Lutz (ed.), *Beyond 1984: Doublespeak in a Post-Orwellian Age* (Champaign-Urbana, IL: National Council of Teachers of English, 1989), 4.
18. Korzybski, 76.

References

Aitchison, Jean. *Language Change: Progress or Decay?* (New York: Universe Books, 1985), 16, 222.

Akmajian, Adrian, Richard D. Demers, Ann K. Farmer, and Robert M. Harnish, *Linguistics: An Introduction to Language and Communication* (3rd ed., Cambridge, MA: MIT Press, 1990), 14, 24.

Andrews, Larry. *Language Exploration and Awareness: A Resource Book for Teachers* (2nd ed., Mahwah, NJ: Lawrence Erlbaum Associates, 1998), 135.

Andrews, Sally. "Spanish Telephone Conventions," in Larry Andrews, *Language Exploration and Awareness: A Resource Book for Teachers* (2nd ed., Mahwah, NJ: Lawrence Erlbaum Associates, 1998), 164.

Anthony, Edward. "The Rhetoric of Behavior," *TESOL Matters* (Vol. 6, No. 5, October/November, 1996), 23.

Barry, Dave. "Mr. Language Person Finds His Nitch," *Lincoln* (NE) *Journal Star*, December 5, 1999.

Baugh, Albert C., and Thomas Cable, *A History of the English Language* (3rd ed., Englewood Cliffs, NJ: Prentice-Hall, 1988), 257.

Brown, Gillian. "The Spoken Language," in Ronald Carter (ed.), *Linguistics and the Teacher* (London: Routledge & Kegan Paul, 1982), 75–76.

Bulley, Michael. "There Ain't No Grammaticality Here," *English Today* (Vol. 15, No. 3, July 1999), 40–41.

Burchfield, Robert. "The Oxford English Dictionary," in Robert Illson (ed.), *Lexicography: An Emerging Profession* (Manchester, England: Manchester University Press, 1986), 19.

Caldwell, Malcom. "Queue & A: The Long and Short of Standing in Line," *The Washington Post National Weekly*, December 21–27, 1992, 38.

Robert G. Carlson, *The Americanization Syndrome: A Quest for Conformity* (New York: St. Martin's Press, 1987), 2.

Carver, Craig M. *American Regional Dialects* (Ann Arbor, MI: University of Michigan Press, 1949).

Cassidy, Frederick G. (ed.), *Dictionary of American Regional English* (Cambridge, MA: Belknap Press of the Harvard University Press, 1985).

Chaika, Elaine. "Discourse Routines," in Virginia P. Clark et al. (eds.), *Language: Introductory Readings* (New York: St. Martin's Press, 1985), 429–455.

Conklin, Nancy Faires and Margaret A. Lourie, *A Host of Tongues: Language Communities in the United States* (New York: Macmillan–The Free Press, 1983), 23, 75–76, 115.

Crabtree, Monica and Joyce Powers. *Language Files* (5th ed., Columbus, OH: Ohio State University Press, 1991), 327, 381.

Crystal, David (ed.). *The Cambridge Encyclopedia of Language* (2nd ed., Cambridge, England: Cambridge University Press, 1997), 23, 35, 52, 53, 88, 112, 290.

Dixon, Robert M. W. *The Rise and Fall of Languages* (Cambridge, UK: Cambridge University Press, 1997), 19, 67, 69, 106.

Edwards, David and Norman Mercer. *Common Knowledge: The Development of Understanding in the Classroom* (London: Heinemann, 1987), 20.

Finegan, Edward and Niko Besnier. *Language: Its Structure and Use* (New York: Harcourt Brace Javanovich, 1989), 341–344, 383.

Fitzgerald, F. Scott. *Tender is the Night* (New York: Charles Scribner's Sons, 1933), 1.

Flexner, Stuart Berg. "'Preface' to the *Dictionary of American Slang*," in Paul Escholz et al. (eds.), *Language Awareness* (4th ed., New York: St. Martin's Press, 1986), 180, 182.

Forestal, Peter. "Talking: Toward Classroom Action," in Marvin Brubaker, Ronald Payne, and Kenneth Ricket (eds.), *Perspectives on*

Small Group Learning: Theory and Practice (Ontario: Rubicon, 1990), 159.

Freeman, Yvonne S. and Freeman, David E. *ENL/EFL Teaching: Principles for Success* (Portsmouth, NH: Heinemann, 1998), 154.

Gere, Ann Ruggles and Eugene Smith, *Attitudes, Language and Change* (Urbana, IL: National Council of Teachers of English, 1979), 8–10.

Grice, Paul. *Studies in the Way of Words* (Cambridge, MA: Harvard University Press, 1989), 26–27.

Halliday, M.A.K. *Learning How to Mean: Explorations in the Development of Language* (London: Edward Arnold, 1975), 37.

Hasselriis, Peter. "From Pearl Harbor to Watergate to Kuwait: Language in Thought and Action," *English Journal* (Vol. 80, No. 2, 1991), 28.

Hayakawa , S. I. and Alan R. Hayakawa. *Language in Thought and Action* (5th ed., New York: Harcourt Brace, 1990), 36–37.

Hendrickson, Robert. *American Talk: the Words and Ways of American Dialects* (New York: Penguin Books, 1987), 25, 25–27, 51–52, 132–133.

Hockett, Charles F. "Logical Considerations in the Study of Animal Communication," in Charles F. Hockett (ed.), *The View from Language* (Athens: The University of Georgia Press).

Hoey, Michael. *On the Surface of Discourse* (London: George Allen & Unwin, 1983), 1.

The Holy Qurían, S.xxx.22.

Hudson, Richard. *Invitation to Linguistics* (Oxford, England: Oxford University Press, 1986), 38.

Hudson, Richard C. "Naming Practices," Language & Culture LIST-SERVE, language-culture@uchicago.edu, July 11, 1995.

Kaplan, Jeffrey. *English Grammar: Principles and Facts* (Englewood Cliffs, NJ: Prentice Hall, 1989), 36.

Korzybski, Alfred. *Science and Sanity: an Introduction to Non-Aristotelian Systems and General Semantics* (4th ed., Lakeville, CT: International Non-Aristotelian Publishing, 1958), 21–22, 34, 76, 92, 389, 452.

Labov, William. *The Social Stratification of English in New York City* (Washington, DC: The Center for Applied Linguistics, 1966).

Labov, William and David Fanshell. *Therapeutic Discourse: Psychotherapy as Conversation* (New York: Academic Press, 1977), 81–82.

Larsen-Freeman, Diane. *Techniques and Principles of Language Teaching* (Oxford, England: Oxford University Press, 1986), 123.

Lass, Roger. *Historical Linguistics and Language Change* (Cambridge, England: Cambridge University Press, 1998), xv.

Lederer, Richard. *The Miracle of English* (New York: Simon & Schuster Pocket Books, 1991), 38–39.

Liu, Dilin and Bryan Farha. "Three Strikes and You're Out," *English Today* (Vol. 12, No. 1, January 1996), 36.

Lutz, William. "Notes Toward a Definition of Doublespeak," in William Lutz (ed.), *Beyond 1984: Doublespeak in a Post-Orwellian Age* (Champaign-Urbana, IL: National Council of Teachers of English, 1989), 4.

Merriam Webster's Collegiate Dictionary (10th ed., Springfield, MA: Merriam-Webster, 1993), 504, 566, 886.

Modiano, Marko. "Standard English(es) and Educational Practices for the World's Lingua Franca," *English Today* (Vol. 15, No. 4, October 1999), 8.

Nienkamp, Jean (ed.). *Plato on Rhetoric and Language* (Mahwah, NJ: Lawrence Erlbaum Associates, 1999), 6–7.

Paulson, Ross Evans. *Language, Science, and Action: Korzybski's General Semantics: A Study in Comparative Intellectual History* (Westport, CT: Greenwood Press, 1983), 87.

Pinker, Steven. *The Language Instinct* (New York: Morrow, 1994), 8, 246.

Piper, Terry. *Language and Learning: The Home and School Years* (Upper Saddle River, NJ: Prentice-Hall, Inc., 1998), 11.

Pooley, Robert C. *The Teaching of English Usage* (Champaign-Urbana, IL: National Council of Teachers of English, 1974), 5.

Postman, Neil. *Crazy Talk, Stupid Talk* (New York: Delacorte Press, 1976), 208, 212.

"Q &A," *The Atlantic Monthly* (Vol. 270, No. 4, October 1992), 14.

Richards, Jack C. *The Language Teaching Matrix* (Cambridge, England: Cambridge University Press, 1990), 68.

Sampson, Geoffrey. *Schools of Linguistics* (London: Century Hutchinson, 1987), 50.

Siegel, Jeff. "Stigmatized and Standardized Varieties in the Classroom: Interference or Separation?", *TESOL Quarterly* (Vol. 33, No. 4, Winter 1999), 701, 702, 721.

Snodgrass, Mary Ellen. *The Great American English Handbook* (Jacksonville, IL: Perma-Bound, 87), 38.

The United Methodist Hymnal (Nashville, TN: The United Methodist Publishing House, 1989).

Trudgill, Peter. *Accent, Dialect, and the School* (London: Edward Arnold, 1975), 35.

Wade-Lewis, Margaret. "The Status of Semantic Items from African Languages in American English," *The Black Scholar* (Vol. 23, No. 26, Summer 1993), 26.

Wallraff, Barbara."Word Court," *The Atlantic Monthly* (Vol, 285, No. 1, January 2000), 132.

West, Fred. *The Way of Language* (New York: Harcourt Brace, 1975), 4.

Widdowson, Henry. *Explorations in Applied Linguistics* (Oxford, England: Oxford University Press, 1989), 138.

Widdowson, Henry. *Teaching Language as Communication* (Oxford, England: Oxford University Press, 1978), 233.

"Wired World Creates New Words," *Lincoln* (NE) *Journal Star*, August 24, 1999, A–4.

Wittgenstein, Ludwig. *The Blue and Brown Books* (New York: Harper Torchbooks, 1960), 28.

Yule, George. *The Study of Language* (Cambridge, England: Cambridge University Press, 1985), 1, 53.

Index

143

428.0071
A567

LINCOLN CHRISTIAN UNIVERSITY   113166

3 4711 00202 4463